MW00996335

The
SOUTHERN PO' BOY

Cookbook

Mouthwatering Sandwich Recipes
from the Heart of New Orleans

The SOUTHERN PO' BOY

Cookbook

Mouthwatering Sandwich Recipes
from the Heart of New Orleans

Todd-Michael St. Pierre

Ulysses Press

Published by:
Ulysses Press
P.O. Box 3440
Berkeley, CA 94703
www.ulyssespress.com

ISBN: 978-1-61243-237-3
Library of Congress Catalog Number 2013938635

Printed in Korea by WE SP Printing through Four Colour Print Group

10 9 8 7 6 5 4 3 2 1

Acquisitions Editor: Kelly Reed
Managing Editor: Claire Chun
Editor: Susan Lang
Proofreader: Elyce Berrigan-Dunlop
Indexer: Sayre Van Young
Front cover design: TG Design
Back cover design, interior design and layout: what!design @ whatweb.com
Photographs: © Judi Swinks Photography
Food stylist: Anna Hartman-Kenzler
Interior illustrations: © Dianne Parks
Background paper image: © donatas1205/shutterstock.com

Distributed by Publishers Group West

For my sister, Mignon... Just because I ♥ U!
And also an extra special thank you to Eric Olsson!

TABLE OF CONTENTS

ACKNOWLEDGMENTS

Merci beaucoup to Fleurty Girl New Orleans for the fantastic exposure! And thanks to the following individuals who each in their own way inspired me or guided the direction of this book: Randall Thomas, Lisa LaFleur, Tracy Babin, Dianne Parks, Laura Godel, May Wen, Anne Lockard, Lolet Boutté, Tricia Boutté-Langlo, Risha Rushing Dunn, Judy Calvin, Patricia V. Combre, Catina Laine, Lynda Church Gaber, and Richard Borja!

INTRODUCTION

"Imagination is the golden-eyed monster that never sleeps. It must be fed; it cannot be ignored." —Patricia A. McKillip

Fantasy author Patricia A. McKillip wasn't referring to the po' boy when she wrote these words, but she very well could have been. Yes, you are limited only by your imagination when it comes to po' boy creation, whether you are a purist who travels the traditional route or an adventurer who is open to the ongoing evolution of this classic Southern marvel of a sandwich. Few things in life have truly earned legend status as much as the humble and mighty New Orleans po' boy.

Hail to the chief of all sandwiches! In a class of its own, it's royal yet down-to-earth and inspires love and devotion. Ask any native of New Orleans where to get the best po' boy, and almost every single person will name a different establishment. Po' boy eateries are as much a part of personal identity as the neighborhood a New Orleanian grew up in. Like a family heirloom, po' boy preference is handed down from generation to generation.

To those of us who love our po' boys, there simply is no substitute for the bona fide best damn sammich on da planet! So if I sing its praises a bit too loudly or go on too long about how mouthwatering it is, and if I dwell on the importance of The Bread and how it has to be crispy and flaky on the outside, unbelievably soft on the inside, to be the real deal, I hope you understand. This is a book for all of us who cherish the po' boy's simple yet sophisticated perfection — although it's just as much a book for po' boy newcomers, who, I know, will love this most magnificent of sandwiches.

This book contains my favorite recipes, including both standards and new twists, for you to make in your own kitchen. Of course, it's always best to enjoy a po' boy in New Orleans, at one of the hundreds of places that cook, serve, and sell the sandwiches. But the taste-tested offerings on these pages will get you started on your journey and show you what to do and how to do it, so you can share po' boys with your friends and family wherever you happen to reside. Explore and get to know your own inner po' boy with a little help from a lifelong po' boy fanatic and native New Orleanian. Bon appetit, y'all!

A SANDWICH WITH A RICH HISTORY

From the very beginning, size was an integral part of the po' boy sandwich. A small po' boy is large by other regions' standards, and in New Orleans large is gigantic. This huge sandwich is history you can eat. The po' boy dates back to 1929, when sandwich-stand owners and brothers Bennie and Clovis Martin offered free overstuffed sandwiches to striking streetcar conductors, whom they referred to as the "poor boys." A letter of support from the Martin brothers promised, "Our meal is free to any members of Division 194." The letter ended, "We are with you till hell freezes, and when it does, we will furnish blankets to keep you warm." (Martin brothers letter courtesy of Louisiana Research Collection, Tulane University Libraries.)

At first, the Martin brothers used regular French bread, but then they asked the folks at John Gendusa Bakery to make the first poor boy loaf, so they would have a better size sandwich bread without narrowed ends to accommodate more filling. Keeping their promise, the Martins provided the striking workers with big, hearty, belly-filling sandwiches. Bennie Martin said, "We fed those men free of charge until the strike ended. Whenever we saw one of the striking men coming, one of us would say, 'Here comes another poor boy.'"

THE PO' BOY TODAY

In the many decades since the Martins fed those striking workers, the po' boy has become New Orleans' signature sandwich. In recent years, it has risen to cult status, with a fanatical following. The po' boy brilliantly sandwiches many of the area's culinary treasures — oysters, shrimp, soft-shell crab, crawfish, andouille sausage, and so much more of the bountiful harvest that is southern Louisiana.

The bread of choice is always local, authentic po' boy bread like a Leidenheimer loaf or other New Orleans–style bread. You can order online if you're out of the area (see Resources on page 101), or you can use a regular loaf of French bread, a baguette, hero or hoagie rolls, or some other bread that appeals to you. I've also included a recipe from my book *Taste of Tremé: Creole, Cajun and Soul Food from New Orleans's Famous Neighborhood of Jazz* (Ulysses Press, 2012) that several food bloggers have raved about. Get creative, because ultimately it's your kitchen and your call. However, you should know that a traditional full po' boy sandwich is about a foot long! If it's "dressed," that means it includes mayonnaise (New Orleanians swear by Blue Plate brand), lettuce, tomato, and pickles. Personally, I like mine lightly dressed or scantily clad. Of course, a dash (or more) of hot sauce — preferably Crystal or Slap Ya Mama brand — can't hurt. And nothing's better with a po' boy than a bag of Zapp's potato chips, a local kettle-cooked favorite.

Just how important is the po' boy to the New Orleans cultural landscape? The humble and mighty po' boy sandwich now has its very own festival: the Oak Street Po' Boy Festival (poboyfest.com), which takes place each November in the Carrollton neighborhood. It features music and food booths, along with a po' boy competition for the city's best creative and traditional po' boy sandwiches. The competition is open to all kinds of cooks, from those running funky mom-and-pop stores to chefs in the fanciest white-tablecloth restaurants.

The unique and awesomely tasty po' boy sandwich is such an important part of the city that its history is included in a permanent exhibit at the Southern Food and Beverage Museum — an essential stop on any tour of New Orleans.

If you can't make it to my hometown sometime soon, you can still get an authentic taste of New Orleans whenever you want, with the help of this book. If you don't already have a passion for po' boys, you surely will once you start making some of the recipes. Enjoy!

BABY, I KNEAD YOU! HOMEMADE PO' BOY BREAD

This is a recipe from my book *Taste of Tremé*. The consensus from my readers and several food bloggers is that this is pretty close to the real thing. So if you want to test your baking skills, try this out.

4 cups all-purpose flour	1 tablespoon salt
1 cup cake flour	2 cups hot water (130°F)
1 packet (2¼ teaspoons) active dry yeast	1 tablespoon unsalted butter
2 tablespoons nonfat dry milk	1 tablespoon cold water
1 tablespoon sugar	

1} In a stand mixer fitted with the paddle attachment, mix together 1 cup of the all-purpose flour and the cake flour, along with the yeast, dry milk, sugar, and salt. Pour in the hot water and butter, mix well, then add remaining flour ½ cup at a time. Near the end of the adding the flour, switch to the dough hook attachment. Add more flour if needed to get to an elastic but not sticky ball of dough. Cover the bowl with a clean kitchen towel and let rest for 12 minutes. Knead on speed 2 for about 12 minutes. The dough should clean the sides of the bowl. Turn out into a lightly oiled bowl with a capacity at least 2½ times the size of the dough. Cover with a clean kitchen towel and let rise until doubled.

2} Punch down the dough and turn it out onto a lightly floured surface. Knead briefly, then divide into 2 pieces. Shape one half at a time into a loose rectangle. Cover loosely and let rest for 12 minutes.

3} Line a rimmed baking sheet with parchment paper. Press and roll each half of the dough into a 10 x 16-inch rectangle. Use your fingers to roll the dough into a 10-inch-long log. Seal the seam and ends. Roll and stretch each log to the length of the longest side of the parchment and place on the prepared baking sheet. Cover loosely with plastic wrap and let rise for 50 minutes. The dough should double easily.

4} Preheat the oven to 400°F. Brush the dough with cold water and use a sharp knife to cut slashes in the top of each log. Place an ovenproof dish on the lowest oven rack and fill the dish with hot water to create steam in the oven; this will help ensure that the crust on your bread is crispy while the inside stays tender. Bake the dough until golden brown, about 35 minutes, rotating the pan halfway through for even color. Cool on a wire rack.

ORIGINAL NOLA

The PEACEMAKER | Fried Shrimp and Oyster Po' Boy

In the late 1800s, in New Orleans and San Francisco, a fried oyster sandwich on a French loaf was known as an "oyster loaf," a term still in use. The sandwich was also called a "peacemaker" or *la mediatrice* ("the mediator") because it was a peace offering brought home to angry wives by husbands who stayed out too late. But it was reborn as the po' boy during the Great Depression, when so many great American sandwiches, including the sloppy Joe, came of age.

Serves 1 to 2

Fried Seafood

canola oil, for frying

2 cups all-purpose flour

1 teaspoon cayenne pepper

1 teaspoon white pepper

1 tablespoon salt

6 large oysters (about 8 ounces)

6 extra-jumbo shrimp (16-20 count)

Slap Ya Mama Dressing

¼ cup mayonnaise

2 to 4 dashes Slap Ya Mama Hot Sauce, to taste

½ teaspoon cayenne pepper

½ teaspoon white pepper

1 teaspoon salt

Assembly

1 (12-inch) French bread loaf, split

fried shrimp and oysters

3 pickle slices

1} Attach a deep-fry thermometer to the side of a 6 to 8-quart cast-iron Dutch oven, and add enough oil to measure 3 inches deep. Over medium heat, heat the oil to 375°F.

2} Meanwhile, make Slap Ya Mama Dressing by combining the mayonnaise and enough Slap Ya Mama Hot Sauce to attain the desired heat level. Add the cayenne pepper, white pepper, and salt. Set aside.

3} Frying the seafood: In a medium bowl, mix together the flour and other dry ingredients. Dredge the oysters and shrimp in the mixture, tap off the excess, and fry until cooked through and golden, about 3 minutes. Fry in batches to avoid crowding. Using a slotted spoon, transfer to paper towels to drain.

4} Spread Slap Ya Mama mayonnaise on one half of the bread, then add the fried seafood and pickles. Close the sandwich, and cut in half to serve.

The KENNER | Ham and Swiss Po' Boy

Oh boy for po' boys! To dress or not to dress? That is the question! If you take your sandwich "dressed," that means it'll come with mayonnaise, lettuce, tomato, and pickles. Personally, I like mine lightly dressed, or scantily clad. Serve with an ice-cold Barq's root beer in a large frosty mug, or of course with a refreshing cold Abita.

Serves 1

2 tablespoons mayonnaise

1 tablespoon Creole mustard

½ teaspoon Louisiana-style hot sauce

1 teaspoon minced fresh garlic

⅔ cup shredded and chilled iceberg lettuce

Assembly

1 (6-inch) French bread loaf, split

4 ounces thinly sliced cooked ham

Cajun or Creole spice, to taste

2 (1-ounce) slices Swiss cheese

⅔ cup lettuce dressing

½ cup chopped tomato

1 } Prepare the lettuce dressing by combining the mayonnaise, mustard, hot sauce, and garlic in a medium bowl. Toss with the lettuce.

2 } Sprinkle the ham with Cajun or Creole seasoning, and heat on a flat grill until hot. Lay the ham on the bottom half of the roll, and immediately top with the Swiss cheese (the ham's heat will soften the cheese). Spread lettuce dressing on the top half of the roll, and add the tomatoes. Fold the roll closed, and serve immediately.

WHO DAT
The
New Orleans–Style BBQ Shrimp Po' Boy

A virtual flavor bomb of New Orleans goodness! Po' boys are purely American in their variety of sauces and condiments, and uniquely NOLA because the shellfish is locally harvested, and as always, they are best served on the crisp and airy local bread.

Serves 4

2 tablespoons canola oil

1 pound extra-jumbo (16-20 count) shrimp, peeled and deveined

2 tablespoon plus 2 teaspoons chopped green onions, both white and green parts

¼ cup dry white wine

1 teaspoon chopped fresh garlic

4 tablespoons Worcestershire sauce

1 teaspoon Tabasco sauce

½ teaspoon cayenne

½ teaspoon paprika

1 cup (2 sticks) butter, cut into small cubes

1 (12-inch loaf) of French bread split nearly apart

1} Preheat a large cast-iron skillet over high heat. Add the oil, and sauté the shrimp just until done, about 2 minutes per side. (It's best to cook the shrimp in batches if you do not have a large skillet.) Remove the cooked shrimp, and set aside.

2} Add the green onions to the hot skillet in which you sautéed the shrimp, and cook for 1 minute. Pour in the white wine, and let simmer until reduced by half. Then add the garlic, Worcestershire sauce, Tabasco sauce, cayenne, and paprika. Shake the pan well, and cook for 1 minute. Reduce the heat to low.

3} Gradually add the cubes of butter, shaking the pan briskly to melt the butter. Continue to add butter and shake the pan until all the butter has melted. Add the shrimp back to the pan, and toss well to coat with the butter and seasonings.

4} Pile the buttered, seasoned shrimp into the loaf, close the sandwich, and cut into four sections to serve.

The JACKSON SQUARE | Muffuletta-Style Po' Boy

This po' boy is a hot mess of genuine deliciousness! Some traditionalists will scoff at the idea of taking the toppings from another of NOLA's signature sandwiches — the Muffuletta (pronounced "muff-a-lotta") — and putting them on po' boy bread, but I must say, the results are quite amazing. If it tastes good, do it. You owe it to yourself (and especially your tongue) to try new things. Peace and chicken grease, y'all!

Serves 4

2 tablespoons mayonnaise

1 tablespoon salad olive juice

2 (12-inch) loaves French bread, split

1 pound hard salami (sliced thin; ask for it to be sliced on #1 at your deli)

1 pound cooked ham (sliced thin; ask for it to be sliced on #1 at your deli)

1½ cups chopped salad olives

8 (1-ounce) slices mozzarella or provolone cheese

1} Preheat the broiler. Place the roll halves, cut side up, on a baking sheet.

2} Combine the mayonnaise and olive juice, and spread the mixture on each roll half. On the bottom half of each roll, layer ham (½ pound), ¾ cup salad olives, and salami (½ pound). Add 2 slices of cheese on the top half of each roll.

3} Set the baking sheet with all the roll halves under the broiler until the cheese has melted and is bubbly, 2 to 3 minutes. Place the cheese halves on top of the meat halves. Cut each in half and serve.

GENTILLY
The

Fish on Fry-Day
Shrimp Po' Boy

When you dig into this one, remember you're biting into the very culinary history of the Big Easy. Po' boys have developed a fanatic following — lovers of NOLA's signature sandwich sing its praises and staunchly defend it as the best of the best.

Serves 2

Fried Shrimp

2½ teaspoons salt

1 teaspoon cayenne pepper

1 teaspoon garlic powder

1 teaspoon paprika

½ teaspoon dried oregano

½ teaspoon dried thyme

½ teaspoon freshly ground black pepper

½ teaspoon onion powder

canola oil, for frying

1½ pounds medium shrimp (36-42 count), peeled and deveined

1 cup buttermilk

1½ cups all-purpose flour

1 cup white cornmeal

Assembly

1 (12-inch) French bread loaf, split

8 tablespoons mayonnaise

2 cups shredded iceberg lettuce

2 medium-sized sliced tomatoes (Creole variety if you can get them)

sliced dill pickles

4-8 dashes Louisiana-style hot sauce (optional)

1} Make a spice mix by whisking together the salt, cayenne, garlic powder, paprika, oregano, thyme, black pepper, and onion powder in a small bowl.

2} Attach a deep-fry thermometer to the side of a 6 to 8-quart cast-iron Dutch oven, and add enough oil to measure 2 inches deep. Over medium heat, heat the oil to 375°F.

3} Place the shrimp and 1 tablespoon of the spice mix in a large bowl, sprinkle over the shimp, and toss to coat. Pour the buttermilk into a medium bowl. Whisk together the flour, cornmeal, and remaining spice mixture in another medium bowl. Dip the seasoned shrimp into the buttermilk, then coat with the flour and cornmeal mixture, tapping off the excess. Working in batches, fry the shrimp until golden brown, about 4 minutes per batch. With a slotted spoon, transfer to paper towels to drain.

4} Spread mayonnaise on each roll half. Place lettuce, tomato, and pickles on the bottom halves of the rolls, and top with the shrimp. Cut the sandwich in half.

5} You can spice things up by adding a few dashes of the hot sauce over the shrimp.

Po' boys have risen to cult status in recent years. How could they not continue to increase in fame and prominence among the hungry masses? Like locals often say, and it's true, po' boys are something of a religious experience!

Serves 2 to 4

Meatballs

1 pound ground beef

1 pound bulk Italian sausage or links removed from casing

1 green bell pepper, diced*

1 yellow onion, diced*

2 stalks celery, diced*

1 jalapeño chile pepper, diced*

1 tablespoon Cajun or Creole spice

1 tablespoon Italian seasoning blend

1 tablespoon garlic powder

1 tablespoon onion powder

2 teaspoons freshly ground black pepper

1 teaspoon paprika

2 large eggs, beaten

1 cup Italian-style bread crumbs

1 cup grated Parmesan cheese

¼ cup heavy cream

8 cloves garlic, minced

* Use half of the diced bell pepper, onion, celery, jalapeño, and garlic to make the meatballs, and reserve the other half for the sauce.

Red Sauce

1 tablespoon extra virgin olive oil

reserved green bell pepper, onion, celery, and jalapeño chile pepper

reserved garlic

2 tablespoons Louisiana-style hot sauce

2 teaspoons Italian seasoning blend

1 teaspoon garlic powder

1 teaspoon onion powder

½ cup chopped fresh Italian parsley

1 (6-ounce) can tomato paste

1 (28-ounce) can crushed tomatoes

3 cups beef broth

3 bay leaves

Assembly

2 (12-inch) loaves French bread (or a hoagie or submarine roll), split nearly apart

1 (8-ounce) package shredded mozzarella cheese

1} Preheat the oven to 375°F.

2} Place the ground beef, sausage, and half of the bell pepper, onion, celery, and jalapeño in a large bowl. Add the Cajun or Creole seasoning, Italian seasoning, garlic powder, onion powder, black pepper, paprika, egg, bread crumbs, cheese, and heavy cream. Add half of the minced garlic. Using your hands, mix all the ingredients well. Dampen your hands, and form the mixture into golf ball–sized meatballs. Place on a lightly greased rimmed baking pan, and bake for 16 to 18 minutes. Remove from the oven, and set aside.

3} Meanwhile, start the sauce by heating the olive oil in a large sauté pan over medium heat. Add the reserved bell pepper, onion, celery, and jalapeño, and sauté for 4 minutes. Toss in the reserved garlic, and sauté 2 more minutes. Add the hot sauce, Italian seasoning, garlic powder, onion powder, and parsley, and cook for 2 more minutes. Add the tomato paste, and cook for 4 minutes. Then add the crushed tomatoes and broth. Toss in the bay leaves, and reduce the heat to low. Cook, uncovered, stirring occasionally, for about 45 minutes. Add the cooked meatballs, along with the pan juices, and cook an additional 40 minutes. Remove the bay leaves.

4} Spoon meatballs and sauce inside the bread, top the filling with mozzarella cheese, and close the sandwich, smashing down a little to melt the cheese. Slice the loaf into 2 to 4 sections, or serve the rolls individually.

Families and friends alike are very often adamantly divided over their allegiance to a particular roast beef po' boy with debris gravy. We Louisianians tend to be quite opinionated on this subject and remain faithful to our favorite po' boy restaurants and delis!

Serves 4 to 8

Roast Beef

1 teaspoon freshly ground black pepper

2 teaspoons onion powder

2 teaspoons garlic powder

1 teaspoon dried thyme

1 (5-pound) bottom round roast

2 medium red onions, quartered

4 medium carrots, halved

4 celery ribs, halved

2 whole garlic heads with skin on, halved

12 cups (3 quarts) beef stock or broth, or enough to cover three-quarters of the roast

Assembly

4 (12-inch) loaves French bread, split nearly apart

mayonnaise

Creole mustard

sliced pickles

1 } Preheat the oven to 350°F.

2 } In a small bowl, combine the black pepper, onion powder, garlic powder, and thyme, and rub the mixture thoroughly over the roast.

3 } Wrap the roast completely in brown paper, using a plain brown paper bag without any printing or ink on it. Place the wrapped roast in a 12 x 10 x 6-inch roasting pan. Scatter the onions, carrots, celery, and garlic on the bottom of the pan. Pour beef stock or broth into the pan until it covers three-quarters of the roast. Place in the oven, and cook until an instant-read thermometer inserted into the thickest part of the roast registers 175°F, or until the outside of the roast begins to fall apart, at least 2½ to 3 hours.

4 } Remove from the oven, let rest for 20 to 25 minutes, and slice as thinly as possible. Strain the pan gravy, and put the sliced roast and the little bits (the debris) back into the pan gravy.

5 } Spread mayonnaise and mustard on both sides of the bread. Pile on generous portions of the roast beef, ladle on lots of debris gravy, and top with pickles. Serve immediately.

PONTCHARTRAIN
The

Pain Perdu (French Toast) Po' Boy

A fun breakfast- or dessert-style po' boy, courtesy of New Orleans: the birth place of jazz and po' boys and far too many other mind-blowing things to count!

Serves 2

Strawberry Jam

12 ounces fresh strawberries, hulled

5 tablespoons sugar, divided

½ teaspoon fresh lemon juice

Pain Perdu

2 eggs

1 cup milk

¼ teaspoon vanilla extract

1 (12-inch) loaf French bread, split nearly apart

2 tablespoons (¼ stick) butter

1 tablespoon vegetable oil

Assembly

½ pound cooked Canadian bacon

strawberry jam

1 teaspoon cinnamon

2 tablespoons powdered sugar

2 tablespoons cane syrup

1} To make strawberry jam, mash the strawberries in a large, wide bowl. In a medium saucepan over low heat, mix together the mashed strawberries, 4 tablespoons sugar, and lemon juice, stirring until the sugar has dissolved. Increase the heat to high, and bring to a full rolling boil. Keep at a boil, stirring often, until the mixture reaches 220°F on an instant-read thermometer, then remove from the heat. Pour into a serving bowl, cover, and refrigerate until needed.

2} Beat the eggs in a bowl or baking dish large enough to submerge the bread in. Add the milk, remaining 1 tablespoon sugar, and vanilla extract, and mix well. Soak the bread in the egg mixture, coating both sides.

3} In a large skillet over medium heat, heat the butter and oil. Fry the bread until golden brown on both sides.

4} Place the bacon on the bottom half of the bread, then top with strawberry jam, cinnamon, and powdered sugar. Add syrup, close the sandwich, and cut into 2 sections to serve.

NOW YOU KNEAUX

The reason we say WHO Dat?

The SAINTS, I thought you KNEW Dat!

Come join the chosen FEW Dat

Do dis like we DO Dat!

And get accustomed TO Dat!

Yeah, you right and TRUE Dat!

For Halloween it's BOO Dat!

For football we say DREW Dat!

For Gumbo we like ROUX Dat!

For Mardi Gras it's KREWE Dat!

Abita Beer, hey BREW Dat!

And Audubon is ZOO Dat!

The reason we say WHO Dat?!?!

The SAINTS, I thought you KNEW Dat!!!

Well, at least . . . Now You Kneaux!

INTERNATIONAL AFFAIRS

"But the truth is something I've said many times, that the best way to describe New Orleans is that if you love them, they will love you back."
—Drew Brees

The ITALIAN | Spicy Italian Sausage Po' Boy

Who says making a po' boy has to be a complicated endeavor? If you like the simple methods best, this is the one for you! It's easy yet succeeds at satisfying even the most insatiable appetites.

Serves 2 to 4

8 (4-ounce) links fresh spicy Italian sausage

1 (26-ounce) jar spaghetti sauce

1 green bell pepper, sliced into strips

1 onion, sliced

Assembly

2 (12-inch) loaves French bread, split nearly apart

Louisiana-style hot sauce

1 (8-ounce) package shredded Italian cheese blend

1} Place the sausage links, spaghetti sauce, bell pepper, and onion in a slow cooker. Stir to coat all the ingredients.

2} Cover and cook on low for 6 hours. Place 4 of the cooked sausages on each loaf of French bread and ladle a generous amount of the sauce over the top. Add hot sauce to taste and as little or as much cheese as desired. Serve immediately.

BYWATER | Eggplant Parmesan Po' Boy

The

The Bywater area of NOLA isn't outside of the U.S. like the other recipes in this International Affairs chapter, but my friend Pam is Italian-American and she lives in the Bywater and she makes this po' boy all of the time! *Seaux* now do you see my logic?! If not, hey, it's still an awesome po' boy.

Serves 4

2 eggs, beaten

1 cup Italian-style bread crumbs

1 eggplant, thinly sliced

1 cup tomato sauce

8 (1-ounce) slices mozzarella cheese

Assembly

4 (6-inch) loaves French bread, split nearly apart

6 pickle spears, sliced

4 leaves romaine lettuce

1} Preheat the oven to 350°F.

2} Place the beaten eggs in a shallow, wide dish, and the bread crumbs on a large plate. Dip the eggplant slices in the egg, and then dredge in the bread crumbs, tapping off the excess. Place in a single layer on an ungreased baking sheet. Bake for 10 minutes on one side, then flip and bake for 5 minutes on the other side.

3} Remove the eggplant from the oven, and transfer to an oiled, 9 x 13-inch glass baking dish. Cover the eggplant slices with the tomato sauce and mozzarella cheese. Bake for 30 minutes.

4} Place the rolls directly on the oven rack to crisp them up for about 3 minutes. Line the bread with pickles and lettuce, and place the baked eggplant on top. Serve immediately.

The SWEDISH
Meatball and Gravy Po' Boy

My friend Eric Olsson of www.redbeansanderic.wordpress.com, foodie extraordinaire and NOLAvore, is of Swedish ancestry and enjoyed the challenge of developing a recipe for this po' boy. First thing I did was test it to make sure it tasted as scrumptious as it sounds, and I'm happy to report that YES it was totally incredible!

Serves 2 to 4

Meatballs and Gravy

8 tablespoons (1 stick) butter, divided

2 tablespoons grated onion

1 pound ground beef

½ pound ground pork

1 egg, beaten

⅔ cup milk

½ cup bread crumbs

1 teaspoon salt

⅛ teaspoon freshly ground black pepper

⅛ teaspoon nutmeg

⅓ cup flour

4 cups beef stock

½ cup sour cream (optional)

Assembly

2 (12-inch) loaves French bread, split nearly apart

2 cups shredded lettuce

2 medium tomatoes, sliced thin

pickle slices

1} In a small sauté pan over medium heat, melt 2 tablespoons of butter and cook the onion until translucent, about 3 minutes. With your hands, mix together the ground meat, sautéed onion, egg, milk, bread crumbs, salt, pepper, and nutmeg in a large bowl. Dampen your hands, and form the mixture into balls about 1 to 1½ inches across (about the size of a golf ball). You should get about 35 to 40 meatballs. Melt 1 tablespoon of butter in a large nonstick pan over medium heat. Brown the meatballs in batches, about 8 to 10 at a time. Add 1 more tablespoon of butter before cooking each batch. Once all the meatballs are nicely browned, put them in a bowl and set aside.

2} To make the gravy, use the same nonstick pan over medium heat. Melt the 6 tablespoons of butter, and then stir in the flour to make a roux. Heat the beef stock in the microwave on high for about 3 minutes. Continuously stir the roux until it has reached a coffee color then slowly mix in the heated beef stock while stirring, and continue until the gravy is smooth.

3} Add all the meatballs to the pan containing the gravy, and simmer on low for 10 minutes. Remove the meatballs to the bowl. If desired, mix sour cream into the gravy, and simmer on low until heated through, about 5 minutes.

4} Place the meatballs on the bottom half of the bread, and dress with lettuce, tomato, and pickle slices, then top with gravy. Nice and messy! For another Swedish touch, you could spread lingonberry jam on the top half of the loaf. Close the sandwich, and slice into 2 sections to serve.

Sugar and spice and everything nice — what girls are made of? Maybe, but sometimes, certain BOYS are too! Ya *kneaux*?!

Serves 4

Pork Roast

1½ cups cold water

4½ tablespoons kosher salt plus more for seasoning, divided

2 tablespoons light brown sugar

4 cloves garlic, smashed

1-inch piece fresh ginger, sliced

4 allspice berries (optional)

½ cup dark rum

2 (12-ounce) pork tenderloins

1 shallot, thinly sliced

¼ head red cabbage, thinly sliced

1 tablespoon roasted peanut oil or extra virgin olive oil

1 tablespoon red wine vinegar

1 tablespoon olive oil

freshly ground black pepper

Assembly

4 (6-inch) hero rolls, split

¼ cup Creole mustard

4 tablespoons mayonnaise or sour cream

sweet pickles

pickled peppers (optional)

4 (1-ounce) slices Swiss cheese

1} Make a brine for the pork by combining the water, 3 tablespoons salt, brown sugar, garlic, ginger, and allspice berries, if using, in a medium saucepan over medium-high heat. Bring to a boil, remove from the heat, and stir in the rum. Cool to room temperature. Place the tenderloins in a wide bowl or shallow container, pour the brine over them, and cover. Alternatively, place the tenderloins and brine in a large Ziploc bag. Refrigerate for at least 1 hour and up to 4 hours.

2} Meanwhile, make the slaw. Soak the shallot in cold water for 5 minutes. Toss together the cabbage, shallot, and 1½ teaspoons salt in a colander set in the sink. Set aside to drain for at least 30 minutes and up to 1 hour. Rinse the cabbage, pat dry, and place in a large bowl. Toss with the peanut or olive oil and vinegar, and season to taste with salt.

3} Preheat a gas or charcoal grill to medium-high heat. Drain and pat the tenderloins dry, then brush with the olive oil and sprinkle with the pepper. Grill the tenderloins, turning as needed to mark all sides. Cook until an instant-read thermometer inserted in the thickest part of the tenderloin registers 145°F, about 8 minutes per side. Set the tenderloins on a cutting board to rest for 5 minutes before thinly slicing.

4} While the meat is resting, place the rolls split side down on the grill, and toast until golden. Brush the bottom half of the toasted rolls with the mustard and mayonnaise or sour cream, and layer on tenderloin slices, pickles, and pickled peppers, if using. On the grill, lightly melt one slice of cheese on the top half of each toasted roll. Place the top halves of the rolls over the bottom halves, and smash down slightly to incorporate the melted cheese. Serve immediately.

By most accounts, the original Martin brothers' free po' boys were filled not with oysters or meat but with a much cheaper carbohydrate combo: french-fried potatoes and brown gravy. You can still get these types of po' boy in The City That Care Forgot. In fact, this is one of my favorites. In her book *Gumbo Tales*, Sara Roahen writes about having to lie down on the floor after eating one: "I could only guess that digestion had usurped all available energies." Truer words have never been written, Sara! Invite the neighbors, unless you don't like them. Regardless, these are worthy of a party.

Serves 2 to 4

canola oil

4 large russet (baking) potatoes cut into ¼ inch slices

1 tablespoon plus 1½ teaspoons unsalted butter, divided

3 tablespoons minced green onion

3 tablespoons fresh thyme

½ cup dry red wine

1 tablespoon water

¾ teaspoon cornstarch

1 cup beef broth

1 teaspoon Kitchen Bouquet

1 tablespoon Worcestershire sauce

1 teaspoon coarsely cracked black pepper

½ teaspoon salt

5 ounces cheese curds

2 tablespoons finely chopped fresh chives

2 (12-inch) loaves French bread, split nearly apart

1} Place an oven rack in the middle position, and preheat the oven to 200°F.

2} Attach a deep-fry thermometer to the side of a 5 to 6-quart heavy pot, and add enough oil to measure 3 inches deep. Over medium heat, heat the oil to 375°F.

3} Peel the potatoes, cut lengthwise into ¼-inch-thick sticks, and submerge in a bowl of ice and cold water. Drain in a colander, then spread in a single layer on paper towels, and pat very dry.

4} Start the gravy by melting 1 tablespoon butter in a small heavy saucepan over medium heat. Add the green onion and thyme, stirring frequently, until the onion is softened and golden, about 2 minutes. Pour in the wine, and bring to a boil. Cook until reduced by half, stirring occasionally, then discard the thyme. While the wine mixture is reducing, stir together the water and cornstarch until the cornstarch has dissolved. Add the beef broth, Kitchen Bouquet, and Worcestershire to the wine, and bring to a boil. Whisk in the cornstarch mixture, and return to a boil. Stir frequently and boil until the sauce is slightly thickened, about 3 minutes. Remove from the heat, and stir in the black pepper, salt, and 1½ teaspoons butter until the butter has melted.

5} Once the oil is at temperature, fry the potatoes in batches, stirring occasionally, until deeply golden, about 6 minutes per batch. Be sure the oil maintains 375°F between batches. With a slotted spoon, transfer the fries to a baking sheet lined with paper towels, and sprinkle lightly with salt. Keep the fries warm in the oven while frying the remaining batches.

6} Spread all the fries on a large ovenproof plate, pan, or dish, sprinkle with the cheese curds, and place in the oven for about 2 minutes, until the cheese is just warmed through. Stir the chives into the gravy, and drizzle over the fries. Warm the bread in the oven, then ladle the poutine into the bread. Close the sandwich, and cut into 2 sections to serve.

The PIZZERIA | Cheesy Pepperoni Po' Boy

Traditional po' boys rule in my book. They need no improving upon — the originals remain the BEST! With that said, it is so fun to explore and invent new renditions and some, like this one, are really delectable. The rules are yours to make or break, so go right ahead. (Like you needed my permission!)

Serves 2 to 4

Pizza Sauce

2 cups water

1 teaspoon dried oregano

1 teaspoon dried basil

3 tablespoons dried parsley flakes

2 cloves garlic

1 (12-ounce) can tomato paste

Assembly

1 (12-inch) loaf French bread, split, buttered, and toasted

8 ounces sliced mushrooms

1 medium red onion, diced

1 large red bell pepper, diced

3 ounces sun-dried tomatoes

1 cup shredded Gouda cheese

1 cup shredded mozzarella cheese

8 ounces pepperoni slices

1} To make the pizza sauce, combine the water, oregano, basil, parsley, garlic, and tomato paste in a small saucepan over medium heat. Cook until the mixture comes to a boil, then reduce the heat to low, and simmer for 10 minutes.

2} Spread a light layer of pizza sauce over the bottom half of the toasted bread. Next, layer on the mushrooms, onion, bell pepper, and tomato. Add the Gouda and mozzarella cheeses. Top with pepperoni and another light layer of pizza sauce. Close the sandwich, and slice into 2 to 4 sections to serve.

MEXICAN
The
Spicy Bean and Taco Po' Boy

These are fun to make with the kids, or those who are kids at heart. Filling and easy too!

Serves 4

Avocado Spread

1 cup sour cream

1 ripe avocado, mashed

Louisiana-style hot sauce, to taste

Filling

1 (16-ounce) can refried beans

1 tablespoon taco seasoning

1 pound thinly sliced deli chicken

Assembly

4 (6-inch) French rolls, split

2 cups shredded cheddar cheese

2 cups shredded lettuce

1 cup diced fresh tomatoes

1 (8-ounce) can sliced black olives, drained

1 red onion, sliced and separated into rings

1 (4-ounce) can diced green chiles

1} In a medium bowl, mix together the sour cream, avocado, and hot sauce until the mixture reaches spreading consistency. Set aside.

2} In a small saucepan over medium heat, heat the refried beans just until warm, then stir in the taco seasoning.

3} Preheat the broiler. Hollow out the bottom halves of the rolls, leaving about a ½ inch of crust for the shell. Place the rolls, cut side up, on a baking sheet. Position about 5 inches from the broiler, and broil until toasted, about 2 minutes.

4} Spread the beans over the bottom halves of the rolls. Top with the chicken, cheese, lettuce, tomato, olives, onion, and chiles. Spread the avocado mixture on the top halves of the rolls. Close the sandwiches, and serve immediately.

The GERMAN | Bratwurst and Mustard Po' Boy

Also known as Berlin on the Bayou, this one goes great with a pint of your favorite dark German beer. Cheers, y'all! Thanks again to Eric Olsson (www.redbeansanderic.wordpress.com) for developing this one.

Serves 2

Bratwurst

1 (16-ounce) beer

2 teaspoons red pepper flakes

1 teaspoon garlic powder

1 teaspoon salt

½ teaspoon freshly ground black pepper

4 links bratwurst

Assembly

2 tablespoons Bavarian-style mustard

2 (6-inch) loaves French bread, split nearly apart

4 (1-ounce) Gouda cheese slices

1 cup sauerkraut

2 tablespoons horseradish sauce

1} In a medium saucepan over medium-high heat, bring the beer, red pepper, garlic powder, salt, and black pepper to a boil. Add the bratwurst, and cook for 10 minutes.

2} Move the bratwurst to either an outdoor grill, grill pan, or stove-top skillet and grill for 10 minutes, turning once. Rub the cooked bratwurst with the mustard.

3} Place the mustard-covered bratwurst in each loaf of bread. Top with the cheese, followed by the sauerkraut and horseradish sauce. Smash down slightly to melt the cheese.

BEIJING
Sweet and Sour Pork Chop Po' Boy

The

Bring a little Asian flair to your town with this tasty take on NOLA's famously flavorful sandwich! I use a good-quality black rice vinegar in this recipe, like Gold Plum's Chinkiang Vinegar, which is similar to balsamic vinegar. Balsamic makes a fine substitute.

Serves 2

2 boneless pork chops, ¾ to 1 inch thick

1 cup chicken broth

¼ cup black rice vinegar

2 tablespoons soy sauce

¼ cup brown sugar

1 small onion, sliced

1 small green bell pepper, sliced into rings

1 (8-ounce) can pineapple chunks, with juice

2 tablespoons cornstarch

2 tablespoons water

2 (6-inch) loaves French bread, split

2 tablespoons finely shredded carrot

1} In a large skillet over high heat, brown the pork chops on both sides. Add the broth, vinegar, soy sauce, brown sugar, onion, bell pepper, and pineapple. Bring to a boil, then reduce the heat to low, cover, and simmer for 1 hour.

2} Add the cornstarch to the water, stirring until smooth. Remove the pork chops from the skillet. Add the cornstarch to the sauce, and cook, stirring, until thickened and clear.

3} Place the pork chops on the bottom half of each loaf. Add the cooked bell pepper and onion. Top with the cooked pineapple and sauce, then the raw shredded carrot. Close the loaves and serve.

The BANGKOK
Squid Po' Boy with Thai Chili Sauce

Squid'ja think I was gonna leave Thailand out? No way! Especially when it becomes a Big Easy po' boy. This one is some GOOD eating.

Serves 2

4 strips peppered bacon

1 (10 to 12-ounce) package frozen breaded calamari

4 tablespoons Thai-style chili sauce

½ cup mayonnaise

2 teaspoons Creole mustard

1 teaspoon minced fresh parsley

2 teaspoons thinly sliced green onion

Assembly

2 (6-inch) sesame hoagie, sub, or French rolls, split nearly apart

1 cup spinach leaves

½ cup julienned red onion

1 teaspoon paprika

1} In a nonstick skillet over medium heat, cook the bacon until crisp and brown on both sides. Drain on paper towels. Once the bacon has cooled, crumble it.

2} Cook the calamari according to package directions.

3} To make the sauce, mix together the chili sauce, mayonnaise, mustard, parsley, and green onion in a small bowl, and set aside.

4} Spread a generous layer of sauce across each side of the roll. Place the spinach on top of the sauce. Pile calamari on top, and sprinkle with bacon crumbles and red onion.

5} Serve the remaining sauce on the side, topped with a sprinkling of paprika.

The VIETNAMESE | Mushroom Bánh Mì Po' Boy

When you're making a po' boy at home and can't get real New Orleans–style French bread, a really good substitute is a bánh mì loaf from a Vietnamese bakery. This bread has a nice mix of soft, chewy, and crunchy. In New Orleans, báhn mì sandwiches are actually called Vietnamese po' boys!

Serves 2

Mushrooms

2 large Portobello mushroom caps

1 tablespoon olive oil

2 teaspoons sea salt

2 teaspoons freshly ground black pepper

Dressing and Sauce

1 carrot, sliced into sticks

1 daikon (white) radish, sliced into sticks

1 cup rice vinegar

1 cup fresh lime juice, divided

½ plus ⅓ cup cold water, divided

2 teaspoons soy sauce

1 teaspoon nuoc mam (Vietnamese fish sauce)

½ teaspoon toasted sesame oil

2 tablespoons canola oil

2 teaspoons minced fresh garlic

⅓ cup granulated sugar

1 (24-inch) baguette, split

1 jalapeño chile pepper, thinly sliced

1 medium cucumber, sliced into long, thin strips

10 leaves fresh Thai basil

½ cup fresh cilantro, chopped

1} Preheat the oven to 450°F. Place the mushroom caps on a baking sheet. Drizzle with the olive oil, and season with salt and pepper. Cook until tender, about 25 minutes. Cool slightly, then slice into strips.

2} While the mushrooms are baking, bring a saucepan of water to a boil. Plunge the carrot and radish sticks into the boiling water, and after a few seconds, remove them and plunge them into a bowl of ice water to stop the cooking. In a medium bowl, stir together the rice vinegar, ½ cup lime juice, and ½ cup cold water. Transfer the carrot and radish to the vinegar and lime marinade, and let soak for at least 15 minutes, longer if it's convenient.

3} To make the sandwich sauce, stir together the remaining ½ cup lime juice and the soy sauce, fish sauce, sesame oil, canola oil, garlic, sugar, and remaining ⅓ cup water in a small bowl.

4} Sprinkle a little of the sauce on each baguette half. Place the mushroom strips on the bottom halves, and sprinkle a little more sauce. Top with jalapeño slices, carrot and radish sticks (minus the marinade), cucumber strips, basil, and cilantro. Close the sandwiches and serve.

The NACHO-YO BOY
Beefy, Cheesy Po' Man

Adult-sized portions make it hard to call these big daddies little boys, so I decided "po' man" would be more appropriate in this case. This is often true with all of these Big Easy gargantuan delights!

Serves 2

Beef Patties

1 pound ground beef

½ small onion, finely diced

pickled jalapeño chile peppers, sliced

2 teaspoons garlic powder

1 (.25-ounce) packet taco seasoning mix

Assembly

1 (12-inch) loaf French bread, split

1 jar chili sauce

1 jar nacho cheese sauce

2 cups shredded lettuce

1 medium tomato, diced

1 bunch green onions, diced

½ cup sour cream

2 cups restaurant-style tortilla strips

1} In a medium bowl, combine the ground beef, onion, jalapeño, garlic powder, and taco mix, using your hands to mix the ingredients. Dampen your hands, split the meat mixture in half and form patties large enough to cover the bread, 2 patties per sandwich. In a large skillet over medium-high heat, cook the patties until cooked through and browned.

2} In separate small pots over low heat, heat the chili sauce until it is warm, and the nacho cheese until it has melted. Place the beef patties on the bottom half of the bread, and layer on the lettuce, tomato, and green onion. Add a few spoonfuls of the chili sauce and nacho cheese. Top with a dollop of sour cream, followed by the tortilla strips. Place the top half of the bread over the filling, and slice into 2 sections to serve.

THE TRUTH REMAINS

Time to feed your soul,

Let the good times roll,

On a beach they call Pontchartrain!

Where Old Man River,

Can still deliver,

A life as sweet as sugarcane!

When the Saints begin,

To go marching in...

Like parades we go marching on . . .

That muddy water,

That old French Quarter,

I know you miss 'em when you're gone!

All the joy and pride,

That you feel inside,

Shines through because the truth remains . . .

You've got NOLA fever,

You're heart just can't leave her . . .

There's café au lait in your veins!

ELEGANT AND FANCY BOYS

"If you're open to it, New Orleans will teach you about yourself, but if you want to hide from who you really are, the city will help you do that, too."

—Laurell K. Hamilton

THE GERT TOWN | Pork Tenderloin Po' Boy

One thing about po' boys—they're loved by all classes of folks down here. Blue collar, white collar, it doesn't matter what part of town you grew up in, it doesn't matter who your daddy was or wasn't, baby: Po' boys are for everybody! Gert Town is a neighborhood in the city of New Orleans. Notable New Orleanians from Gert Town include singers Merry Clayton and Tami Lynn, and musician-composer Allen Toussaint.

Serves 4

Pork Tenderloin

5 teaspoons Cajun or Creole seasoning

2 (12-ounce) pork tenderloins

1 tablespoon olive oil

1 teaspoon red wine vinegar or apple cider vinegar

¼ teaspoon salt

¼ teaspoon cracked black pepper

¼ teaspoon dried thyme

Rémoulade Sauce

¾ cup mayonnaise

2 tablespoons Creole mustard

2 teaspoons Worcestershire sauce

2 teaspoons finely minced fresh parsley

1 teaspoon Cajun or Creole seasoning

½ teaspoon dried minced garlic

¼ teaspoon dried minced onion

salt and pepper, to taste

Assembly

2 (12-inch) loaves French bread, split

½ head iceberg lettuce, shredded

2 tomatoes, thinly sliced

1} Preheat a charcoal grill to high heat.

2} To make the rémoulade sauce, whisk together the mayonnaise, mustard, Worcestershire sauce, parsley, Cajun or Creole seasoning, garlic, onion, and salt and pepper, cover, and refrigerate for 1 to 2 hours.

3} Rub Cajun or Creole seasoning all over the pork tenderloins. When the grill is at temperature, cook the tenderloins, turning often to brown all sides, until an instant-read thermometer inserted into the thickest part of the tenderloins registers at a temperature of 145°F, about 25 minutes. Remove from the grill, and let rest on a raised rack for 15 minutes. Slice very thinly.

4} To make the dressing, whisk together the oil, vinegar, salt, black pepper, and thyme. Toss with the shredded lettuce. Lay the two loaves of bread split side down on the grill, and toast them until golden. Place the dressed lettuce on the bottom halves of the bread, and layer on the tomato and pork. Slather the top halves of the bread generously with rémoulade sauce. Close the loaves, and cut each in half to make 4 sandwiches. Serve immediately.

ALGIERS BOY
The

Fried Scallop and Chipotle Po' Boy

You'll know you're consuming this sandwich properly when you have delicious juices running down to your elbows and chipotle mayonnaise in your hair. Just sayin'.

Serves 2

Scallops

2 cups peanut oil, for frying

1 pound large sea scallops (10-15 count) per po' boy

1 teaspoon sea salt

1 teaspoon white pepper

1 cup Italian-style bread crumbs

Chipotle Sauce

¾ cup mayonnaise

juice of ½ lemon

1 large chipotle chile pepper in adobo sauce (in Mexican section)

Assembly

1 (12-inch) French baguette, split

thinly sliced tomatoes

½ cup shredded red cabbage

1} In a 6-quart cast-iron pot, preheat the oil to 375°F, using an instant-read thermometer to check the temperature.

2} To make the chipotle mayonnaise, blend the mayonnaise, lemon juice, and chipotle in a food processor or blender.

3} Season the scallops with the salt and pepper. Place the bread crumbs on a plate, and dredge the scallops, tapping off the excess. When the oil is at temperature, fry the scallops, in batches to avoid crowding, until golden brown. Do not overcook them!

4} Spread chipotle mayonnaise on both halves of the bread. Layer tomato slices and scallops on the bottom half of the bread, and drizzle more mayonnaise over top. Cover with red cabbage, and then place the other half of the bread on top. Cut into 2 sections to serve.

The TUSCAN
Hot Monte Cristo Po' Boy

A simple and easy concoction that your taste buds will salute you for. Nothing fancy, just VERY good. Great served with a café au lait!

Serves 1

1 link hot Louisiana pork sausage

2 (1-ounce) slices Swiss cheese

4 tablespoons grape or strawberry jelly

1 (6-inch) loaf French bread, split nearly apart, buttered, and toasted

1} Split the sausage down the center, and butterfly it (spread it out flat). In a large skillet over medium heat, pan-fry the sausage until cooked through, about 3 minutes on each side. Once the sausage is cooked, place the slices of Swiss cheese over it.

2} Meanwhile, spread the jelly on both sides of the crispy, toasted bread. Once the cheese has melted, place the sausage and cheese in the loaf. Serve immediately.

These sandwiches just seem to have a way of turning folks, tourists, and natives into evangelists, possessed by the urge to spread the po' boy gospel.

Serves 1 to 2

Mushrooms

¼ cup olive oil

1 clove garlic, minced

¼ teaspoon onion powder

1 teaspoon salt

½ teaspoon freshly ground black pepper

pinch of cayenne pepper

¼ cup roasted red peppers

1 (8-ounce) package shredded Parmesan cheese

2 or 3 portobello mushroom caps

Assembly

1 (12-inch) loaf French bread, split

provolone cheese

balsamic vinegar

1} Preheat the oven to 350°F.

2} To make the filling for the mushroom caps, combine the olive oil, garlic, onion powder, salt, black pepper, cayenne, roasted red peppers, and ½ of the Parmesan cheese in a small bowl.

3} Line a baking pan with aluminum foil, and spray with nonstick cooking spray. Place the mushrooms rounded side down. Spoon the filling into each mushroom cap. Bake for 7 to 10 minutes. Turn the oven to broil. Sprinkle the remaining Parmesan cheese over each mushroom, and broil for another 2 to 3 minutes, or until the cheese bubbles.

4} Place the stuffed mushrooms on the bottom half of the bread, top with the provolone cheese, and drizzle with balsamic vinegar. Close the sandwich, smashing down slightly to melt the provolone, and slice into 2 sections. Serve immediately.

The original po' boys were sandwiches made of leftover bits of roast beef and gravy or sliced potatoes and gravy on French bread and were sold to the general public for a nickel. Seems only natural to me that the delicious fillings have evolved into anything imaginable these days!

Serves 1

Trout

egg wash (½ cup milk and 1 egg)

1 (10-ounce) rainbow trout fillet with skin removed

1 cup pecan crust (recipe below)

Pecan Crust

½ cup panko bread crumbs

½ cup toasted chopped pecans

¼ tablespoon sliced fresh chives

⅛ tablespoon minced fresh thyme

1 clove garlic, minced

2 tablespoons unsalted butter, melted

1 teaspoon kosher salt

½ teaspoon freshly ground black pepper

Meunière Sauce

6 tablespoons (¾ stick) unsalted butter, ½-inch dice, at room temperature, divided

1 tablespoon flour

1 cup clam juice

⅓ cup Worcestershire sauce

1 teaspoon Tony Chachere's Creole Seasoning or other Cajun or Creole seasoning

1 clove garlic, minced

1 (12-inch) French roll, split

1} To make the pecan crust, combine the bread crumbs, pecans, chives, thyme, garlic, melted butter, salt, and black pepper in a medium bowl.

2} In a small bowl, whisk together the egg and milk to make an egg wash. Lightly brush the egg wash on the flesh side of the trout, and pack the pecan crust on that side of the fillet until completely covered. Set aside.

3} To make the meunière sauce, preheat a small sauté pan over medium heat. Add 2 tablespoons softened butter (reserve the remaining butter to finish the sauce) and all the flour to the pan, and stir with a whisk for 1 minute to create a blond roux. Slowly add the clam juice, whisking constantly. Stir in the Worcestershire sauce, Tony Chachere's, and garlic. Turn off the heat, and fold in the remaining butter.

4} In a medium nonstick sauté pan over medium-high heat, place the fillet, crusted side down, and cook two thirds of the way, about 6 minutes. Carefully flip the fillet with a spatula to crisp the skin side, about 4 minutes.

5} Place the trout fillet on the bottom half of the bread, and cover with mèuniere sauce to make a good and messy sandwich! Serve immediately.

The West Bank of New Orleans is just across the Mississippi from the city, and it includes towns like Algiers, Terrytown, Gretna, Harvey, Marrero, and Westwego. Proud residents often refer to the West Bank as the Best Bank!

Serves 2

Shrimp and Artichokes

½ cup cornmeal

½ cup rice flour

¼ cup sesame seeds

pinch of cayenne pepper

salt, to taste

1 cup milk

canola oil, for frying

4 large quartered artichoke hearts

1 pound jumbo (16-20 count) shrimp (optional)

Coleslaw

1 cup shredded carrot

¼ head red cabbage, shredded

¼ head green cabbage, shredded and chopped

2 tablespoons mayonnaise

¼ cup red wine vinegar

1 teaspoon celery seed

1 teaspoon garlic powder

2 teaspoons freshly ground black pepper

2 tablespoons agave syrup

Assembly

2 (6-inch) loaves French bread or 2 (5-inch) kaiser rolls, split

1} To make the coleslaw, toss together the carrot and both cabbages in a large container. In a small bowl, whisk together the mayonnaise, vinegar, celery seed, garlic powder, black pepper, and agave syrup. Add to the vegetables, toss well, cover, and chill in the refrigerator for at least an hour.

2} In a clean small bowl, thoroughly mix together the cornmeal, rice flour, sesame seeds, cayenne, and salt. Pour the milk into another small bowl.

3} Attach a deep-fry thermometer to the side of a 6 to 8-quart cast-iron Dutch oven, and add enough oil to measure 2 inches deep. Dunk the artichoke hearts in the milk, shake off the excess, and coat in the flour mixture. Fry in batches. Each side should cook for about 1½ to 2 minutes. Using a slotted spoon, transfer to paper towels to drain. Repeat with the shrimp, if using.

4} Pile coleslaw into the bread, and top with the artichokes and shrimp, if using.

The BENNY | Eggs Benedict Po' Boy

What could be better than this NOLA breakfast to kick your day off right or to refuel and replish yourself after a night of French Quarter–style drinking and debauchery? In fact, the perfect *combeaux* is one of these with a spicy, Cajun-style Bloody Mary for breakfast or brunch. You'll enjoy it so much that you'll soon forget you ever had a hangover, just in time to hit the pavement and do it all over again! Thanks to Eric Olsson (www.redbeansanderic.wordpress.com).

Serves 2

Hollandaise

2 egg yolks

2 tablespoons fresh lemon juice

¼ teaspoon cayenne pepper

1 tablespoon red wine vinegar

½ cup (1 stick) butter, cut into small cubes

Poached eggs

2 tablespoons white vinegar

3 or 4 eggs

Assembly

1 (12-inch) loaf French bread, split and toasted

Canadian bacon or bacon strips

1 tablespoon chopped fresh chives

1} In a nonstick skillet over medium-high heat, cook the bacon until crisp on both sides. Remove and drain on paper towels.

2} To make the hollandaise sauce, whisk together the egg yolks, lemon juice, cayenne, and red wine vinegar in a small saucepan over low heat. Turn the heat to medium, slowly add the butter, and whisk until the butter and the eggs are thoroughly blended. If the sauce separates, add 2 teaspoons of water and continue to whisk until it thickens.

3} To poach the eggs, bring a sauté pan (wide enough to accommodate all the eggs without crowding) of water (about 2 inches) to a simmer over medium heat until water temperature is 180°F, and add the white vinegar. The water should never boil. Crack an egg into a cup and carefully slide it into the liquid. Repeat quickly with the remaining eggs. Cook the eggs until the whites are firm and the yolks nearly done, about 3 minutes.

4} Meanwhile, spread a little of the hollandaise sauce on the bottom half of the toasted bread, and top with the bacon. When the eggs are done, remove them with a slotted spoon to drain the liquid, and place them over the bacon. Top with more hollandaise sauce, and sprinkle on the chives. Serve the top half of the loaf with butter, cane syrup, or your favorite jam or jelly.

If you've ever seen the stately Southern mansions that grace the tree-lined boulevard known as St. Charles Avenue in New Orleans, then you probably understand why I named this luxurious po' boy after such an elegant thoroughfare. It's an appropriately uptown kind of sandwich, with juicy lobster tails breaded in Creole seasoning and two kinds of mustard, deep-fried until perfectly golden brown, and then doused in a succulent serving of rémoulade.

Serves 4

Lobster Tails

canola oil, for frying

1 cup yellow cornmeal

1 cup self-rising flour

1 tablespoon Cajun or Creole seasoning

2 tablespoons garlic powder

2 eggs

1 cup milk

1 teaspoon hot sauce

2 tablespoons Creole mustard

1 tablespoon yellow mustard

4 (10-ounce) frozen lobster tails with shell on, thawed, shelled, and halved lengthwise

kosher salt

freshly ground black pepper

Rémoulade Sauce

1½ tablespoons yellow mustard

1½ cups mayonnaise

1 tablespoon Worcestershire sauce

1 tablespoon paprika

⅛ teaspoon garlic salt

1½ tablespoons horseradish

1½ teaspoons hot sauce

2 tablespoons white wine vinegar

¼ cup finely chopped fresh parsley

kosher salt and freshly ground black pepper, to taste

Assembly

4 (6-inch) club rolls, split

2 large tomatoes, sliced

1} Attach a deep-fry thermometer to the side of a 6 to 8-quart cast-iron Dutch oven, and add enough oil to measure 3 inches deep. Over medium heat, heat the oil to 375°F.

2} In a shallow dish, mix together the cornmeal, flour, Cajun or Creole seasoning, and garlic powder. In a medium bowl, whisk together the eggs, milk, hot sauce, and both mustards.

3} Season each lobster tail with a light sprinkle of salt and pepper. Dredge the lobster in the egg mixture and then in the cornmeal and flour breading, tapping off the excess. Place into the hot oil, and cook for just about 6 minutes, until crisp and golden. Drain on paper towels.

4} Place all the ingredients for the rémoulade sauce in a food processor, and blend until smooth. The sauce is best when blended the night before and allowed to sit overnight in a covered container in the fridge.

5} Divide the lobster among the rolls, and top with tomato slices and rémoulade sauce.

PACIFIC NORTHWEST
The

Baked Salmon with Wasabi Mayo Po' Boy

The great thing about the innovative spirit of the po' boy is that it lends itself to such a vast and versatile spectrum. Regardless of where you reside, you can use local ingredients to give the sandwich a regional personality and create what suits your fancy! The only real criteria is that you make it delicious so it's worthy of the sacred title of po' boy!

Serves 4

Baked Salmon

2 tablespoons (¼ stick) melted butter

3 tablespoons sesame oil, divided

1 (2-pound) salmon fillet

¼ teaspoon salt

¼ teaspoon freshly ground black pepper

Wasabi Mayonnaise

⅓ cup mayonnaise

1½ teaspoons fresh lemon juice

1 teaspoon prepared wasabi

Assembly

2 (12-inch) loaves French bread, split

4 green onions, chopped

2 tablespoons toasted sesame seeds

1} Preheat the oven to 425°F.

2} Drizzle the butter and 2 tablespoons sesame oil into a 13 x 9-inch baking dish, tilting the dish to coat the bottom. Place the salmon in the dish, and brush with the remaining oil. Sprinkle salt and pepper over the top. Bake, uncovered, for 18 to 22 minutes, or until the fish flakes easily with a fork.

3} Meanwhile, make the wasabi mayo by combining the mayonnaise, lemon juice, and wasabi in a small bowl. Set aside.

4} Remove the salmon from the oven, and sprinkle with the green onion and sesame seeds. Place on the bottom half of the bread, cover with wasabi mayo, and close the sandwich. Cut each sandwich into 2 sections to serve.

A sandwich with such humble beginnings as the po' boy comes dressed with many stories. Yes, these poor boys have such a rich history! You could also use sirloin steak instead of beef tenderloin for this fancy boy.

Serves 2

Steak

2 (8-ounce) center-cut beef tenderloin steaks

4 tablespoons cracked black pepper

1 tablespoon plus ½ teaspoon kosher salt, divided

1 tablespoon olive oil

1 tablespoon butter

Cream Sauce

6 ounces cremini mushrooms

2 tablespoons butter

1 shallot, minced

1 clove garlic, minced

1 cup heavy cream

1 teaspoon freshly ground black pepper

1 tablespoon chopped basil

Assembly

2 (6-inch) French rolls, split and slightly toasted

1} Season the tenderloins with the cracked black pepper and 1 tablespoon salt. In a large sauté pan over medium-high heat, heat the oil and 1 tablespoon butter. Place the tenderloins in the pan, and cook for 4 minutes, then turn and cook for 3 minutes. Transfer to a plate, cover with foil, and set aside.

2} To start the cream sauce, slice the mushrooms, and set aside. In a clean large saucepan over medium-high heat, heat 2 tablespoons of butter. Add the shallot and mushrooms, and sauté for 2 minutes. Toss in the garlic, and sauté until it softens, about 3 minutes. Add the heavy cream and steak juice from set-aside plate, and reduce by one-third, until the sauce thickens and coats the back of a spoon. Season with ground black pepper and ½ teaspoon salt, and add the basil. Keep warm over very low heat.

3} Slice the tenderloins thinly, and place slices on the bottom halves of the rolls, and spoon warm cream sauce over the beef. Close the sandwich and serve immediately.

THE UNUSUAL BOYS

"To get to New Orleans you don't pass through anywhere else. That geographical location, being aloof, lets it hold onto the ritual of its own pace more than other places that have to keep up with the progress."

—Allen Toussaint

TERREBONNE | Fried Alligator Tail Po' Boy

Try the gator, it won't bite! Exotic? Yes, but readily available online through www.cajungrocer.com. Happy tailgating! Who Dat!

Serves 2

1 pound alligator tail meat, cut into ½-inch cubes

1 cup buttermilk

¼ cup packaged seasoned fish fry

¼ teaspoon salt

¼ teaspoon freshly ground black pepper

peanut oil, for frying

Assembly

4 tablespoons mayonnaise

3 tablespoons Zatarain's Creole Mustard

1 (12-inch) loaf French bread, split nearly apart

4 tomato slices

¾ cup shredded lettuce

1} Soak the gator meat in the buttermilk for an hour, then drain. Place the seasoned fish fry, salt, and black pepper in a plastic bag, and add the gator meat. Toss until the meat is thoroughly coated with batter.

2} Attach a deep-fry thermometer to the side of a 6 to 8-quart cast-iron Dutch oven, and add enough oil to measure 3 inches deep. Over medium heat, heat the oil to 360°F. Fry the gator until the cubes float, then transfer to paper towels to drain.

3} Spread the mayonnaise and mustard on the bottom half of the bread. Add the tomato, then the gator meat, and top with the shredded lettuce. Cut into 2 sections to serve.

THE 9TH WARD
Chicken Tender Po' Boy with Creamy Creole Mustard Sauce

Creole flavor is often imitated but seldom replicated, and in this case the secret really is in the sauce! I would say "enjoy," but I'm figuring that might be redundant since I already expect you will!

Serves 2 to 4

Chicken

1 pound chicken breast tenders

½ teaspoon salt

½ teaspoon freshly ground black pepper

Creamy Creole Mustard Sauce

1 tablespoon minced shallots

2 tablespoons cider vinegar

½ teaspoon cracked black pepper

1 small bay leaf

½ cup dry white wine

½ cup heavy cream

1 cup (2 sticks) unsalted butter, softened

¼ cup Creole mustard

2 tablespoons Dijon mustard

2 tablespoons Gulden's Spicy Brown Mustard

Assembly

1 (24-inch) baguette, split

2 cups mixed greens

1 large diced tomato

4 ounces mushrooms (optional)

4 (1-ounce) slices cheese (optional)

1} Preheat the oven to 350°F.

2} To make the creamy Creole mustard sauce, combine the shallot, vinegar, cracked black pepper, bay leaf, and wine in a medium pot over high heat. Reduce the mixture to about ¾ cup. Add the cream and reduce by half. Strain the sauce and return to the heat. Add the butter gradually, whisking it over low heat. Stir in all 3 mustards.

3} Bake the chicken tenders uncovered on a broiling pan for 10 to 15 minutes, or until cooked through. Heat the baguette in the oven directly on the rack until crisp, about 5 minutes.

4} Dress the baguette halves with the sauce, and place mixed greens on the bottom half of the bread. Layer on the tomato and then the chicken. Add the mushrooms and cheese, if using, and close the sandwich. Cut in half to serve.

ATCHAFALAYA

The

Crawfish Étouffée
Po' Boy

Follow instructions for this delicious crawfish étouffée, and simply spread it on New Orleans French Bread or the bread of your choice. Traditional étouffée is a Cajun/Creole stew that starts with a roux and usually includes some type of seafood. It sometimes has a tomato base, depending on which part of Louisiana it's from, and is typically served over rice. You can order frozen Louisiana crawfish tails at www.cajungrocer.com, or they may be available at your local grocery store.

Serves 1 to 2

1 cup (2 sticks) butter

1 cup finely chopped white onion

½ cup finely chopped celery

1 cup finely chopped green onion

2 teaspoons minced fresh garlic

2 tablespoons flour

1 (14-ounce) can whole cherry tomatoes

2 fish bouillon cubes

2 cups water

2 teaspoons salt

1 teaspoon freshly ground black pepper

dash of cayenne

1 tablespoon Worcestershire sauce

1½ cups crawfish tails, rinsed and drained

1 (12-inch) loaf French bread, split

1} In a large saucepan over medium-high heat, melt the butter. Sauté the onion, celery, and green onion until tender, about 5 minutes. Toss in the garlic, and cook 2 additional minutes. Add the flour, stirring constantly until it turns golden brown, about 15 minutes. Add the tomatoes and cook an additional 5 minutes until they are incorporated into the roux. Boil the water and add the bouillon, cooking until dissolved. Add the liquid to the roux, stirring constantly. Simmer for about 12 minutes. Add the salt, black pepper, cayenne, Worcestershire sauce, and crawfish. Cook for an additional 20 minutes, stirring occasionally.

2} Brown the split French bread under the broiler. Spoon the crawfish étouffée over the bottom half of the bread, cover with the top half, and cut into 2 sections to serve. This can also be cut into smaller pieces and served as an appetizer at your next finger-food party.

The TEXAN
Barbecue Brisket Po' Boy

They say things are bigger in Texas, and this Tex-ana-style po' boy doesn't disappoint in that regard. If you can't eat it all in one sitting, worry not — simply save the other half for another meal, or bring it to a friend, canine or otherwise!

Serves 6 to 9

Brisket

1 (4 to 5-pound) fresh (not corned) beef brisket

1½ cups cold water

½ cup Worcestershire sauce

2 tablespoons cider vinegar

2 cloves garlic, minced

1½ teaspoons beef bouillon granules

1½ teaspoons chili powder

1 teaspoon ground mustard

½ teaspoon cayenne pepper

¼ teaspoon garlic salt

Sauce

1 cup ketchup

3 tablespoons brown sugar

2 tablespoons (¼ stick) butter

1 teaspoon hot sauce

Assembly

3 (12-inch) loaves French bread, split nearly apart

1} Cut the brisket in half, and place in a 5-quart slow cooker. In a small bowl, combine the water, Worcestershire sauce, vinegar, garlic, bouillon, chili powder, mustard, cayenne, and garlic salt. Reserve ½ cup of the mixture for the sauce, refrigerating it in a small container. Pour the remaining mixture over the beef. Cover and cook on low for 8 to 10 hours, or until the meat is tender.

2} Remove the beef, and skim the fat from the cooking juices. Shred the slightly cooled meat with two forks, return to the slow cooker, and heat through.

3} To make the sauce, in a small saucepan over medium high heat, combine the ketchup, brown sugar, butter, hot sauce, and reserved mixture you refrigerated. Bring to a boil, then reduce the heat to low. Simmer, uncovered, for 4 minutes.

4} Spoon 1 pound of the beef into each loaf, and drizzle sauce over the top. Close the loaves, and slice each in 2 to 3 sections to serve. Save the leftover beef for more sandwiches.

JOSEPHINE

The

Creole-Style Sloppy Joe Po' Girl

Did you know that NOLA's Leidenheimer Baking Company produces one million pounds of genuine po' boy bread annually? And their delivery trucks are marked with slogans like, "Sink ya teeth into a piece of New Orleans cultcha," or "There's no SUBstitute for a REAL New Orleans Po' Boy."

Serves 2 to 3

Sloppy Joe

1 pound ground sirloin beef

¼ cup diced onion

¼ cup diced green bell pepper

⅛ cup finely diced jalapeño chile pepper

1 teaspoon salt

¼ teaspoon pepper

¼ teaspoon Cajun or Creole seasoning

1 cup ketchup

3 teaspoons brown sugar

1 teaspoon Creole mustard

1 tablespoon Worcestershire sauce

½ cup water

Assembly

1 (12-inch) loaf French bread, split nearly apart

2 to 3 tablespoons mayonnaise

1 cup shredded lettuce

1 medium tomato, sliced

sliced dill pickles

1} In a large skillet over medium-high heat, brown the ground beef. Add the onion, bell pepper, and jalapeño, stirring occasionally, about 10 minutes. Drain off the fat if necessary. Stir the salt, pepper, Cajun or Creole seasoning, ketchup, brown sugar, Creole mustard, Worcestershire sauce, and water into the ground beef mixture, making sure to combine well. Reduce the heat to low, cover, and cook for 20 minutes.

2} Spread mayonnaise on both sides of the bread, and line the bottom half of the loaf with the lettuce, tomato, and pickle. Pile on the meat mixture, close the sandwich, and cut into 2 to 3 sections to serve.

The PLAQUEMINES

Turkey and Stuffing Thanksgiving Po' Boy

This is what to do with all those delicious Turkey Day leftovers! You'll give thanks for this Crescent City culinary creation, long after the third Thursday in November has come and gone.

Serves 2

3 tablespoons mayonnaise

1 (12-inch) loaf French bread, split

2 tablespoons mustard

¾ cups cranberry sauce

1 to 1½ pounds turkey meat

1½ cups stuffing

½ cup giblet gravy

1} Spread the mayonnaise on the bottom half of the bread and mustard on the top. Spread the cranberry sauce across the bottom half of the bread. Layer the turkey meat and stuffing over the cranberry sauce. Drizzle the gravy over the dressing, close the sandwich, cut into 2 sections, and serve.

The LAFAYETTE | Boudin Po' Boy

Acadiana (Cajun French; l'Acadiane) is the official name given to the French Louisiana region that is home to a large Cajun/Francophone population. Of the 64 parishes that make up the state of Louisiana, 22 named parishes are in this region. Boudin blanc is the traditional boudin of the area, and it's also the one most widely consumed. Also popular are alligator boudin, crawfish boudin, and seafood boudin consisting of crab, shrimp, and rice. Be a genuine swamp person, and *geaux* get you some real Cajun Boudin, the sausage of Acadiana, at www.cajungrocer.com.

Serves 2

4 (4-ounce) links boudin

4 (1-ounce) slices pepper jack cheese

2 (6-inch) French rolls, split

1} To steam-cook the boudin, place the links in a steamer basket set over a pot of boiling water. Steam for 3 to 5 minutes on high heat, then turn heat down to low and cook an additional 10 minutes, or until the internal temperature reaches 160°F on an instant-read thermometer. Turn off the heat and let the sausage stand for 2 minutes.

2} Place the cheese on the bread and place under the oven broiler until it is melted. Unwrap the boudin, split and remove the casing, and place the link on the bread. Serve immediately.

The PHILLY | The Rib Eye Steak Mississippi Po' Boy

This one comes from a friend in Philadelphia, Mississippi, and it's certain to be blasphemous and pure sacrilege in the other Philadelphia, but we like it just fine down here.

Serves 4

1 large clove garlic, cut in half

2 choice rib eye steaks, ¾ inch thick

1 tablespoon Cajun or Creole seasoning

2 teaspoons freshly ground black pepper

1 medium red bell pepper, cut in half lengthwise with core, seeds, and membrane removed.

1 small red onion, cut into ¼ -inch-thick slices

4 (6-inch) hoagie or club rolls, split nearly apart

8 (1-ounce) slices provolone cheese, quartered

1} Spray the grate of an outdoor grill and utensils with nonstick spray, and preheat the grill to high. Meanwhile, rub the garlic all over the steak, and season both sides with the Cajun or Creole seasoning and black pepper.

2} Place the steak, bell pepper, and onion on the heated grill. Cook the steak for 3 minutes on one side and then 3 minutes on the other for a medium-rare steak (internal temperature 130°F) or 5 minutes per side for medium (140°F). Remove from the grill, cover with foil to keep warm, and let stand for 10 minutes.

3} While you're cooking the steaks also grill the vegetables until the pepper is slightly blackened and the onion is tender. Remove the onions from the grill to a cutting board. Place the bell pepper in a plastic bag, and let stand for 1 to 2 minutes until the skin loosens and is cool enough to handle. Peel the skin from the pepper, and cut it and the onion into thin strips.

4} Place the rolls on the grill face side down, and toast until golden brown. Be careful not to burn the bread if the grate is still very hot. Carve the steak into thin slices, place on the bread, and top with bell pepper, onion, and cheese. Put the po' boy on the grill over indirect heat (not directly over the coals). Cover the grill for 2 to 3 minutes until the cheese is melted. You can also melt the cheese under the oven broiler. Close the rolls, and serve immediately.

Monday means red beans and rice, and on Tuesday they taste twice as nice! Here's a nontraditional take on a classic NOLA meal. You'll probably have some beans left over so, cook you up some rice tomorrow or the next day and have yourself some more beans. You know what they always say, "dey better da second day, cher!" Cher is an endearing Cajun word that is often used in place of "dear."

Serves 2

- 1 pound dried red beans
- 8 ounces shredded pork (see directions for cooking a larger pork roast)
- 1 teaspoon olive oil or bacon drippings
- 1 onion, diced
- 1 green bell pepper, diced
- 4 ribs celery, diced
- ¼ teaspoon minced fresh garlic
- 4 cups water
- 2 tablespoons crushed red pepper
- 1 tablespoon Cajun or Creole seasoning
- ¼ cup chopped fresh parsley
- 1 pound andouille sausage
- 1 (12-inch) loaf French bread, split nearly apart
- Creole mustard

1} Soak the red beans overnight in a bowl of water, remove any floating beans, and then rinse and drain.

2} To get 8 ounces of shredded pork, cook a pork roast of the desired size in a crock pot on low for the length of time recommended in the appliance directions. Once the pork has finished cooking, shred the whole roast or just 8 ounces of it with two forks. Use the rest for a meal or leftovers.

3} In a sauté pan over medium-high, heat the oil or bacon drippings. Sauté the onion, bell pepper, celery, and garlic, stirring occasionally, for 10 minutes. Meanwhile, in a large pot over high heat, bring the drained beans and 4 cups fresh water to a boil. As the water reaches a boil, the vegetables should be finished. Add them to the boiling pot. Reduce the heat to low, and simmer for 45 minutes. Then stir in the shredded pork, crushed red peppers, and Cajun or Creole seasoning, and simmer for another 45 minutes.

4} Remove a cup of the red beans, mash them, and return them to the pot to cook for another 30 minutes. During this last half hour, check the red beans. If water remains in the pot, mash up some more beans and blend them in. Right before serving, stir in the parsley.

5} Split the sausage down the center, and butterfly it (spread it out flat). In a large skillet over medium-high heat, pan-fry the sausage until cooked through, about 8 minutes on each side.

6} Place the sausage on the bread. Top with the thickened red bean mixture, and top with Creole mustard. Cut into 2 sections, and serve immediately.

The BUFFALEAUX | Buffalo Wing with Blue Cheese Po' Boy

Shuffle off to New Orleans with this delicious offering. Even if you can't always be there in real life, you can enjoy the flavor of this incredible city at home. (Oh, and go right on ahead and feel free to cook and/or dine in the buff. No one has to know!)

Serves 4 to 6

Hot Chicken Strips

8 (3-ounce) frozen, breaded chicken strips

4 tablespoons (½ stick) butter

½ cup Crystal Hot Sauce

Dressing

½ cup crumbled blue cheese

½ cup mayonnaise

6 tablespoons milk

Assembly

2 (12-inch) loaves French bread, split nearly apart

12 slices Creole or beefsteak tomato

4 (12-inch) stalks of celery, sliced into thin sticks

1} Preheat the oven to 375°F.

2} Place the frozen chicken fingers on a baking pan, and bake according to package directions. Remove from the oven, and transfer to a medium bowl.

3} In a small saucepan over medium heat, melt the butter with the hot sauce. Cook for 2 minutes while stirring. Pour the butter and hot sauce mixture over the chicken, and toss to coat.

4} In a small bowl, combine the blue cheese, mayonnaise, and milk. Whisk until smooth.

5} Place slices of tomato and the celery sticks on the bottom half of each loaf. Next, place the chicken fingers over the tomato and celery, and top with a generous drizzle of the blue cheese dressing. Close the sandwiches, cut each loaf into 2 to 3 sections, and serve.

The SLIDELL | Ultimate BLT Po' Boy

This takes your standard BLT and infuses it with gourmet flavor for a tenacious twist. But no one will have to twist your arm to eat it; I will promise you that! Slidell is a city in the greater New Orleans metropolitan area that is often considered a suburb. It is located on the northeast side of Lake Pontchartrain close to the Mississippi border.

Serves 2

1 medium tomato, sliced

1½ teaspoons olive oil

1 clove garlic, minced

2 sprigs fresh thyme

½ teaspoon salt

¼ teaspoon freshly ground black pepper

4 slices thick-cut smoked applewood bacon

1 cup mayonnaise

¼ cup fresh basil

1 (12-inch) loaf French Bread, split and toasted

1 cup arugula

4 (1-ounce) slices mozzarella cheese (optional)

1} Preheat the oven to 200°F. Line a 9 x 13-inch baking or roasting pan with aluminum foil. Spread the tomato slices across the foil. Whisk together the oil, garlic, thyme, salt, and black pepper, and pour over the tomatoes. Bake for 45 minutes, or until the edges of the tomatoes start to caramelize.

2} Meanwhile, in a nonstick skillet over medium heat, cook the bacon, turning frequently, until crisp and brown on both sides. Drain on paper towels.

3} Combine the mayonnaise and basil in a small bowl, mixing well. Spread the mixture on both halves of the bread, then layer with the arugula, caramelized tomato slices, and bacon. Top with mozzarella cheese, if desired. Close the sandwich, and cut into 2 sections to serve.

The po' boy to me is "bayou blissfulness," and trust me, it would be completely unacceptable to describe NOLA's famous and fabulous food with any other phrase. If you're the adventurous type, why not ask a local what po' boy they would suggest and then visit a hole in the wall, small neighborhood, or corner bar. That way you'll get to experience some true and traditional po' boy culture, plus you're bound to also be converted into a devout and fervent follower of that establishment. No time for neighborhood haunts? Most restaurants in NOLA also serve up a mean po' boy (actually it's hard to find a bad one in the city), and you'll have this book to guide you in further exploration when you get back home.

Serves 2

Rémoulade Sauce

1 cup mayonnaise

3 tablespoons dill relish

2 tablespoons fresh chopped parsley

2 tablespoons fresh chopped chives

2 tablespoons chopped capers

2 teaspoons Creole mustard

1½ teaspoons chopped shallot

1 teaspoon Louisiana-style hot sauce

Tomatoes

peanut oil, for frying

1 egg

1 cup milk

1 cup flour

1½ cups cornmeal

1 teaspoon salt

1 teaspoon freshly ground black pepper

2 medium green tomatoes sliced about ⅓ inch thick

Shrimp

1 tablespoon olive oil

1 tablespoon Cajun or Creole seasoning

1 pound jumbo (16-20 count) shrimp, peeled and deveined

Assembly

1 (12-inch) baguette, split

1 cup shredded lettuce

1} To make the rémoulade sauce, combine the mayonnaise, relish, parsley, chives, capers, mustard, shallot, and hot sauce in a small bowl, mixing well. Cover and chill. For best results, prepare the night before.

2} Attach a deep-fry thermometer to the side of a 6 to 8-quart cast-iron Dutch oven, and add enough oil to measure 2 inches deep. Over medium heat, heat the oil to 350°F.

3} In a small bowl, whisk together the egg and milk to make an egg wash. Place the flour in another small bowl. Combine the cornmeal, salt, and black pepper in a third small bowl. Dredge the tomato slices in the flour, dip in the egg wash, and coat in the cornmeal mixture, tapping off the excess. Drop the battered tomato slices in the hot oil, and fry until golden brown, 3 to 5 minutes on each side. With a slotted spoon, transfer to paper towels to drain.

4} In a medium bowl, combine the olive oil and Cajun or Creole seasoning. Coat the shrimp in the mixture. In a large nonstick frying pan over high heat, sauté until cooked through, about 2 to 3 minutes per side. Shrimp will turn pink and be firm to the touch when done.

5} Place the cooked fried green tomato slices on the bottom half of the baguette, and layer the shrimp over the tomato, covering the entire half. Top with lettuce and then drizzle the rémoulade sauce over the lettuce. Cut into 2 sections, and serve immediately.

The MAMA'S BOY | Glazed Ham with Macaroni and Cheese

As a proud mama's boy, I speak from experience when I tell you this is one hell of a sensational Sunday supper. Thanks, Mama!

Serves 8 to 12

Glazed Ham

1 (8-pound) ready-to-eat smoked ham

1 cup brown sugar

2 tablespoons golden syrup

4½ tablespoons flour, divided

½ teaspoon cinnamon

2 tablespoons Creole mustard

1 tablespoon cider vinegar

2 tablespoons pineapple juice

Mac 'n' Cheese

2 (7¼-ounce) boxes macaroni & cheese dinner

2 teaspoons salt

2 teaspoons freshly ground black pepper

2 teaspoons Cajun or Creole seasoning

8 tablespoons (1 stick) butter, cut into small cubes

3 cups shredded cheddar cheese

2 cups milk

Assembly

4 (12-inch) loaves French bread, split

2 to 3 tablespoons mayonnaise

2 cups shredded lettuce

4 medium tomatoes, sliced

2 tablespoons Creole mustard

1} Preheat the oven to 350°F.

2} Line a roasting pan with aluminum foil. Wrap the ham in foil, and place in the pan. Reheat until an instant-read thermometer inserted into the thickest part of the ham registers 145°F, about 20 minutes per pound. Remove the ham from the foil, trim off any excess fat, and score a diamond pattern over the surface.

3} Meanwhile, make a glaze by combining the brown sugar, syrup, 2 tablespoons flour, cinnamon, mustard, and vinegar in a medium saucepan over medium heat. Cook, stirring constantly, until the mixture is smooth, about 8 minutes. Then add the pineapple juice. When the mixture begins to lightly boil, reduce the heat to simmer, and continue stirring for another minute.

4} Baste the scored ham with the glaze mixture, and return it to the oven. Periodically baste the ham with more glaze until the ham reaches an internal temp of 160°F. Remove from the oven, let stand for 20 minutes, and carve slices for the sandwiches.

5} Cook the mac 'n' cheese according to package directions.

6} In a small bowl, combine the remaining 2½ tablespoons flour with the salt, pepper, and Cajun or Creole seasoning. Grease a 4-quart baking dish, and pour half of the cooked mac 'n' cheese in. Sprinkle half of the flour mixture over the mac 'n' cheese, and top with half of the butter and half of the cheese. Repeat with the remaining mac 'n' cheese, flour mixture, butter, and cheese. Pour the milk over the top. Cover with aluminum foil, and bake at 350°F for 35 minutes. Remove the foil, and bake uncovered for an additional 10 minutes.

7} Spread the mayonnaise across the bottom half of the bread. Layer with slices of glazed ham followed by a layer of baked mac 'n' cheese. Dress with lettuce, tomato, and Creole mustard, smash down slightly, and slice into 2 to 3 sections to serve.

BAYOU ST. JOHN
Charbroiled Oyster Po' Boy

"I've been all over the world. I love New York, I love Paris, San Francisco, so many places. But there's no place like New Orleans. It's got the best food. It's got the best music. It's got the best people. It's got the most fun stuff to do." — Harry Connick, Jr.

Serves 2 to 6

½ cup (1 stick) unsalted butter, very soft

1 pinch sea salt

1 teaspoon freshly ground black pepper

1 tablespoon minced fresh garlic

4 tablespoons grated pecorino Romano cheese, plus more for topping

pinch of cayenne

pinch of white pepper

squirt of fresh lemon juice

1 teaspoon minced Italian parsley

12 freshly shucked large oysters on the half shell (increase number if they are small- or medium-sized)

1 (12-inch) loaf French bread, split

1} Preheat an outdoor grill until very hot. Meanwhile, make a buttery cheese sauce by mixing together the softened butter, salt, black pepper, garlic, 4 tablespoons of the cheese, cayenne, white pepper, lemon juice, and parsley in a food processor. Pulse until smooth.

2} Place the oysters, shell side down, on the hottest part of the grill, and let them cook in their own juices until they begin to bubble and their edges curl, 2 to 3 minutes. Do not overcook! Add a dab of the buttery cheese sauce on each oyster a minute or 2 before removing them from the grill. Lay the bread split side down on the grill, and toast until golden.

3} Remove the oysters from the shells, and place on the bottom half of the bread. Sprinkle some pecorino Romano cheese over thr top, close the sandwich, and cut into 2 sections for a meal to serve. Divide into 6 sections for appetizers.

MY CITY

This is for my city, for the passion that grows inside . . .

For Old Man River's holy waters, muddy, deep, and wide!

The moss-draped, ancient oaks of Audubon and City Park . . .

The skyline from the Algiers' Ferry after dark!

This is for my city, and to her fierce will to survive . . .

Came damn near close to drowning, bet your brass she's still alive!

The carriage rides and streetcars, depth of character and joy . . .

A Mardi Gras of memories that time just can't destroy!

The best food and music! A jazzy jewel of the South . . .

She's divine and delicious! Curse her not! Yeah, watch ya mouth!

This is for my city, with flaws and all, She brings me pride . . .

For Old Man River's holy waters . . .

Muddy,

Deep,

and

Wide!

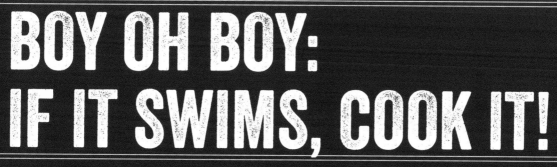

BOY OH BOY:
IF IT SWIMS, COOK IT!

"New Orleans, more than many places I know, actually tangibly lives its culture. It's not just a residual of life; it's a part of life. Music is at every major milestone of our life: birth, marriage, death. It's our culture."

—Wendell Pierce

The TREMÉ | Fried Catfish Po' Boy

The now-famous Tremé neighborhood of New Orleans is famous for lots of things, like being the actual birthplace of jazz, and that same jazzy rhythm has seemingly made its way into the food the folks there cook and serve on a daily basis. This catfish po' boy is one testament to that glorious truth!

Serves 4

½ cup buttermilk

1 teaspoon Tabasco sauce

½ teaspoon salt

¼ teaspoon cayenne pepper

¼ cup yellow cornmeal

¼ cup flour

2 teaspoons Cajun or Creole seasoning

¼ teaspoon minced fresh garlic

3 tablespoons canola oil, divided

4 (6-ounce) catfish fillets

Assembly

4 (6-inch) French rolls, split

½ bottle Louisiana-style tartar sauce

2 cups shredded lettuce

1 large Creole or beefsteak tomato, sliced

1} Whisk together the buttermilk, Tabasco, salt, and cayenne in a medium bowl. In a large shallow dish, stir together the cornmeal, flour, Cajun or Creole seasoning, and garlic.

2} In a large skillet over medium heat, heat half of the oil. Dip two catfish fillets into the buttermilk mixture, and dredge in the cornmeal and flour mixture, tapping off the excess. Fry the fillets until golden brown, turning once, about 6 minutes. Heat the remaining oil, and repeat the procedure for coating and cooking the other 2 fillets.

3} Spread tartar sauce on both sides of the rolls. Layer on lettuce and tomato slices on each roll, and top with a catfish fillet. Serve immediately.

In the Deep South, deep frying is still considered the number one technique for cooking seafood. You can expect to eat seafood in this manner when visiting Cajun country (everything in moderation, of course). This recipe makes enough that you can invite old and new friends over to help you devour these mighty tasty po' boys!

Serves 6

Fried Oysters

peanut oil, for frying

1 egg

1 cup milk

1 cup water

2 tablespoons Creole mustard

1 tablespoon yellow mustard

salt and cracked black pepper, to taste

1½ cups yellow cornmeal

1½ cups yellow corn flour

2 tablespoons garlic powder

4 dozen fresh oysters

Assembly

6 (6-inch) loaves French bread, split

3 cups Rémoulade Coleslaw (recipe follows)

18 thin slices tomato

spicy ketchup

1} Preheat the oven to 375°F. Place the bread on a large cookie sheet, and set aside.

2} Attach a deep-fry thermometer to the side of a 6 to 8-quart cast-iron Dutch oven, and add enough oil to measure 3 inches deep. Over medium-high heat, heat the oil to 375°F. Adjust heat to maintain this temperature.

3} Meanwhile, make the rémoulade coleslaw (page 50), and set aside.

4} Make an egg wash by whisking together the egg, milk, water, both mustards, and salt and pepper in a medium bowl. In a separate medium bowl, combine the cornmeal, corn flour, and garlic powder. Dip the oysters, 6 at a time, in the egg batter and then into the cornmeal and corn flour mixture, tapping off the excess. Drop into the hot oil, and cook until the oysters float, about 3 minutes. Remove with a slotted spoon, and drain on paper towels.

5} While the oysters are frying, place the bread in the preheated oven, and turn off the heat, to allow the bread to become warm and crispy. Remove from the oven, and place rémoulade coleslaw and tomato slices on the bottom halves of the bread, and spicy ketchup on the top halves. Lay 6 oysters over the coleslaw, close the sandwiches, secure with toothpicks, and slice each in half. Serve immediately.

Rémoulade Coleslaw

1½ cups mayonnaise

½ cup Creole mustard

1 tablespoon Worcestershire sauce

1 teaspoon Louisiana-style hot sauce

½ cup spicy ketchup

¼ cup minced red bell pepper

¼ cup minced banana pepper

½ cup minced celery

3 tablespoons minced fresh garlic

¼ cup minced fresh parsley

½ tablespoon fresh lemon juice

salt and cracked black pepper, to taste

1½ cups shredded green cabbage

1½ cup shredded red cabbage

¾ cup finely shredded carrots

1} To make this spicy rémoulade sauce, combine the mayonnaise, mustard, Worcestershire sauce, hot sauce, ketchup, bell pepper, banana pepper, celery, garlic, parsley, lemon juice, and salt and pepper, mixing well. Toss together the shredded cabbages and carrot, then add the rémoulade sauce, tossing well to combine.

This is my personal all-time favorite po' boy — nothing else comes close! When it comes to a specific regional food item that makes me think of home and brings back memories of my family and our traditions, this po' boy reigns supreme. It's a NOLA thing!

Serves 4

Fried Soft-Shell Crab

1 egg

1 cup milk

1½ cups flour

1 tablespoon baking powder

8 (3½-inch) soft-shelled crabs, cleaned

1 tablespoon salt

2 teaspoons freshly ground black pepper

peanut oil, for frying

Assembly

2 (12-inch) loaves French bread, split and toasted

4 to 6 tablespoons mayonnaise or tartar sauce

4 cups shredded iceberg lettuce

pickle slices

3 medium tomatoes, sliced

Louisiana-style hot sauce, to taste

1} In a medium bowl, make an egg wash by whisking together the egg and milk. In another medium bowl, sift together the flour and baking powder.

2} Season the crabs with salt and pepper. Dip the crabs in the egg wash, and then dredge in the flour mixture, tapping off the excess. Set aside.

3} In a large frying pan over medium high heat, pour enough oil to measure 1½ inches deep, and heat to 350°F. Carefully drop the battered crabs into the hot oil, but do not crowd the pan. Fry in batches until golden brown, turning once, about 5 minutes on each side. Drain on paper towels.

4} If you want a crispier French loaf, split each and brown under the broiler until toasted. It is recommended that you not crisp the outside of the loaf. Dress each loaf with mayonnaise or tartar sauce, lettuce, and pickle and tomato slices. Place 4 crabs on each loaf, and season with a dash or two of hot sauce. Close the loaf and cut each into 2 sections. Serve immediately.

Crab Imperial meets NOLA po' boy bread. It's an incredible combination you'll be making again and again. And much like a streetcar ride down St. Charles Avenue through New Orleans's spellbinding Garden District, this one's not just good, it's bordering perfection!

Serves 6

6 tablespoons (¾ stick) unsalted butter, divided

3 tablespoons flour

2 cups heavy cream

1 pound jumbo lump crabmeat, drained and picked over for shell pieces

1 cup Italian-style bread crumbs, divided

½ cup finely chopped red bell pepper

¼ cup finely chopped red onion

4 tablespoons finely chopped parsley, divided

2 tablespoons sherry

2 tablespoons fresh lime juice

1½ teaspoons Worcestershire sauce

1 teaspoon paprika, divided

1 teaspoon dry mustard

½ teaspoon cayenne pepper

salt and freshly ground black pepper, to taste

3 (6-inch) submarine or hoagie rolls, split

1} Preheat the oven to 400°F.

2} In a medium saucepan over medium-high heat, melt 4 tablespoons butter. Add the flour, and cook, stirring, until smooth, approximately 2 minutes. Whisk in the heavy cream, and bring to a boil. Reduce the heat to medium, and cook, stirring, until thickened, about 10 minutes.

3} Remove from the heat, and stir in the crabmeat, half the bread crumbs, bell pepper, onion, half the parsley, sherry, lime juice, Worcestershire, half the paprika, mustard, cayenne, and salt and pepper. Divide the mixture evenly among 6 shallow 6-ounce ramekins (oval if you have them). Place the ramekins on a baking pan, and set aside.

4} In a small bowl, mix the remaining 2 tablespoons butter with the remaining bread crumbs and paprika until evenly combined. Sprinkle the mixture evenly over the ramekins. Bake until lightly browned and bubbling in the center, about 20 minutes.

5} Remove from the oven, and sprinkle with the remaining parsley. Set the broiler to low, and toast the bread for about 2 minutes. Spoon the contents of 2 ramekins onto each roll. Cut in half and serve immediately. Serve immediately.

THE HARAHAN
Oyster Po' Boy with Bacon and Blue Cheese

You can't get any more New Orleans than this if you try! My favorite fish fry for this one is Zatarain's Seasoned Fish-Fri, which you can find in many national grocers or online, but use what you can get, or the one you like best.

Serves 1

Fried Oysters

peanut oil, for frying

3 strips bacon

10 medium oysters

1 (10-ounce) package premixed seasoned fish fry

Assembly

1 (8-inch) hoagie or submarine roll, split

1 tablespoon mayonnaise

3 ounces shredded lettuce

3 slices tomato

crumbled blue cheese

Louisiana-style hot sauce

1} Attach a deep-fry thermometer to the side of a 6 to 8-quart cast-iron Dutch oven, and add enough oil to measure 3 inches deep. Over medium heat, heat the oil to 375°F.

2} Meanwhile, in a nonstick skillet over medium heat, cook the bacon until crisp on both sides. Drain on paper towels.

3} Coat the oysters with seasoned fish fry according to package directions. When the oil reaches temperature, fry the battered oysters until golden, about 2 minutes. Don't crowd the pot, but fry in batches, about 5 oysters at a time. Remove with a slotted spoon, and drain on paper towels.

4} Spread mayonnaise on the bread, and layer on the lettuce, tomato, and cheese. Add the bacon, and top with the oysters. For an extra kick, add a few dashes of hot sauce.

The MARIGNY | Cajun Tilapia Po' Boy

This one is pretty easy, so don't worry about being perfect. Just do what I do… drink way too many glasses of wine while cooking and call it all "close enough!"

Serves 2

Fish Strips

½ cup flour

1 tablespoon Cajun or Creole seasoning

3 (6-ounce) tilapia fillets, quartered lengthwise

2 tablespoons canola oil

Assembly

1 (12-inch) baguette, split

¼ cup mayonnaise

1 cup shredded lettuce

16 pickle chips

Louisiana-style hot sauce

1} In a shallow bowl, combine the flour and Cajun or Creole seasoning. Coat the tilapia with the flour mixture, tapping off the excess. Heat about ½ inch of oil in a large nonstick skillet over medium heat. To avoid crowding, cook the tilapia in batches until cooked through, 4 minutes per side.

2} Spread the mayonnaise on both sides of the baguette. Add the lettuce, pickle chips, and tilapia, and sprinkle on hot sauce. Cut into 2 sections, and serve immediately.

SATCHMO
The
Creole Crab Cakes Po' Boy

Bring your BIG boy and girl appetites with you when you come to New Orleans to hunt down a legendary po' boy: A full sandwich is about 12 inches long! The purists rightfully insist it isn't really a po' boy if the bread isn't true New Orleans French bread, which is what I use to make all of the sandwiches in this book. However, feel free to enjoy all of these NOLA flavors on whatever bread you so choose. It will still taste like the Big Easy — just don't let the po' boy mafia of Orleans parish find out. They're adamant about the bread, as am I, but hey, you use what you have! Still, the real-deal is always the best and authentic choice for me.

Serves 2 to 4

Crab Cakes

2 tablespoons plus 2 teaspoons mayonnaise

2 tablespoons plus 2 teaspoons Creole mustard

¼ cup chopped red bell pepper

2 tablespoons chopped green onion

2 teaspoons grated lemon zest

1 teaspoon Cajun or Creole seasoning

8 ounces lump crabmeat, cleaned and drained

½ cup crushed unsalted saltine crackers (about 13), divided

4 tablespoons light olive oil

Assembly

1 (12-inch) loaf French bread, split

1½ cups shredded lettuce

1 red onion, thinly sliced

1 } Blend together the mayonnaise and mustard, then mix with the bell pepper, green onion, lemon zest, and Cajun or Creole seasoning. Carefully pick any shell fragments from the crab that may remain, making sure the lumps stay intact. Gently stir in the crabmeat, trying not to break up the crab pieces, and ¼ cup cracker crumbs. Form 4 (3-inch) patties, and coat with the remaining crumbs. Refrigerate for 30 minutes.

2 } In a large nonstick skillet over medium heat, heat the oil. Cook the patties, turning once, until browned, 3 to 4 minutes per side. Drain on paper towels. Place the lettuce, onion, and crab cakes on the bread. Cut into 2 to 4 sections and serve.

> "You get a line and I'll get a pole, honey,
> You get a line and I'll get a pole, babe.
> You get a line and I'll get a pole,
> We'll go fishin' in the crawdad hole,
> Honey, baby mine."
> — *Old Cajun Song*

Serves 4

Fried Crawfish Tails

vegetable oil, for frying

1 cup cornmeal

½ cup all-purpose flour

2 teaspoons Cajun or Creole seasoning

1 teaspoon salt

1 teaspoon freshly ground black pepper

1 cup buttermilk

2 teaspoons Louisiana-style hot sauce

1 (16-ounce) package crawfish tails, rinsed and drained

Rémoulade Sauce

1 cup mayonnaise

3 tablespoons dill relish

2 tablespoons fresh chopped parsley

2 tablespoons fresh chopped chives

2 tablespoons chopped capers

2 teaspoons Creole mustard

1½ teaspoons chopped shallot

1 teaspoon Louisiana-style hot sauce

Assembly

4 (6-inch) hoagie rolls, split

shredded green leaf lettuce

1} To make the rémoulade sauce, combine the mayonnaise, relish, parsley, chives, capers, mustard, shallot, and hot sauce in a small bowl, mixing well. Cover and chill. For best results, prepare the night before.

2} Attach a deep-fry thermometer to the side of a 6 to 8-quart cast-iron Dutch oven, and add enough oil to measure 2 inches deep. Over medium heat, heat the oil to 350°F.

3} In a medium bowl, combine the cornmeal, flour, Cajun or Creole seasoning, salt, and pepper. In a separate medium bowl, combine the buttermilk and hot sauce. Soak the crawfish tails in the buttermilk mixture for 10 minutes, then dredge the tails in the flour mixture, tapping off the excess. To avoid crowding, fry the crawfish in batches until golden brown, about 3 minutes per batch. Drain on paper towels.

4} Serve on hoagie rolls with shredded lettuce and rémoulade sauce.

"I was just mind-blown to find that New Orleans is just so much more fun and interesting than I had ever thought." — Harold Perrineau

Serves 4

Blackening Mix

1 teaspoon dried oregano

1 teaspoon dried thyme

1 teaspoon dried parsley

1 teaspoon dried rosemary

1 teaspoon dried basil

1 teaspoon garlic powder

1 teaspoon onion powder

1 teaspoon ground black pepper

1 teaspoon sea salt

4 teaspoons paprika

½ teaspoon Cajun or Creole seasoning

½ teaspoon cayenne powder

Blackened Shrimp

blackening mix

1½ pounds large (31-35 count) shrimp, peeled and deveined

Assembly

4 (6-inch) French rolls, split

8 slices bacon

2 tablespoons mayonnaise

1 cup thinly shredded red cabbage

3 thick slices ripe tomato, cut in half

salt and freshly ground black pepper, to taste

½ cup crumbled feta cheese

1} Preheat a medium cast-iron skillet over medium heat. Cook the bacon, turning occasionally, until crisp on both sides, about 8 minutes. Drain on paper towels.

2} While the bacon cooks, thoroughly combine all the blackening mix ingredients in a medium bowl. Rinse the shrimp and pat dry, then add to the bowl with the blackening mix, and toss very well to coat the shrimp evenly.

3} Spoon out all but 1 tablespoon of bacon grease from the skillet, and increase the heat to high, until the grease just barely starts to smoke. Add the shrimp and stir-fry until done, 4 to 6 minutes. Remove to a bowl, and cover with foil to keep warm.

4} Crumble the cooked bacon. Spread a thin layer of mayonnaise on both sides of the bread. On the bottom half of each French roll, layer on red cabbage, 2 tomato half slices, salt and pepper, bacon crumbles, shrimp, and feta cheese. Serve immediately.

RESOURCES

AUTHENTIC PO' BOY BREAD

www.cajungrocer.com

www.nolacajun.com

www.cajunsupermarket.com

BOUDIN AND OTHER CAJUN SPECIALTY MEATS

www.comeaux.com

www.beststopinscott.com
Based in Scott, Louisiana (near Lafayette), this website has the most impressive variety and selection I have seen and they ship anyplace.

Jacob's World Famous Andouille (www.cajunsausage.com)

LOCAL BRICK-AND-MORTAR GROCERY STORES

These are my favorite places in south Louisiana for "makin' groceries" (buying all the food and supplies I need).

Rouses (www.rouses.com)

LeBlanc's (www.leblancsfoodstores.com)

Langensteins (www.langensteins.com)

Breaux Mart (www.breauxmart.com)

Dorignac's (www.dorignacs.com)

Tony's Seafood Market (www.tonyseafood.com)
In Baton Rouge, Tony's is Louisiana's largest seafood market, featuring fresh seasonal seafood, packed and shipped nationwide. They also carry bulk spices and seasonings.

OTHER FAVORITES

Tony Chachere (www.tonychachere.com)
Down in Louisiana, this is a popular brand for a wide variety of products. It's often found in stores nationwide or can be ordered directly from their website.

Zatarains (www.zatarains.com)
Also often found at supermarkets across the country.

The New Orleans School of Cooking's Louisiana General Store (www.nosoc.com)
The school's store sells lots of products that they ship.

Zapp's Potato Chips (www.zapps.com)
Of course, po' boys go best with our local and much loved kettle-cooked Zapp's, which come in a wide variety of flavors.

Abita Beer (www.abita.com)
And these Louisiana boys are even better washed down with our locally brewed Abita Beer (Amber, Purple Haze, and Turbo Dog, to name a few flavors). You'll find Abita at several national chains, including Trader Joe's.

MEASUREMENTS AND SUBSTITUTIONS

COMMON EQUIVALENTS

1 gallon = 4 quarts = 8 pints = 16 cups =128 fluid ounces = 3.8 liters

1 quart = 2 pints = 4 cups = 32 ounces = .95 liter

1 pint = 2 cups = 16 ounces = 480 ml

1 cup = 8 ounces = 240 ml

¼ cup = 4 tablespoons = 12 teaspoons = 2 ounces = 60 ml

1 tablespoon = 3 teaspoons = ½ fluid ounce = 15 ml

TEMPERATURE CONVERSIONS

Fahrenheit (°F)	Celsius (°C)
200°F	95°C
225°F	110°C
250°F	120°C
275°F	135°C
300°F	150°C
325°F	165°C
350°F	175°C
375°F	190°C
400°F	200°C
425°F	220°C
450°F	230°C
475°F	245°C

VOLUME CONVERSIONS

U.S.	U.S.	Metric
1 tablespoon	½ fluid ounce	15 ml
¼ cup	2 fluid ounces	60 ml
⅓ cup	3 fluid ounces	90 ml
½ cup	4 fluid ounces	120 ml
⅔ cup	5 fluid ounces	150 ml
¾ cup	6 fluid ounces	180 ml
1 cup	8 fluid ounces	240 ml
2 cups	16 fluid ounces	480 ml

WEIGHT

U.S.	Metric
½ ounce	15 grams
1 ounce	30 grams
2 ounces	60 grams
¼ pound	115 grams
⅓ pound	150 grams
½ pound	225 grams
¾ pound	350 grams
1 pound	450 grams

INDEX

Po' boy names/nicknames and major ingredients, as well as individual recipes included in po' boy instructions, are indexed. Spices, garnishes, optional ingredients, and the everpresent lettuce, tomatoes, pickles, and bread, are not indexed.

ABOUT THE AUTHOR

© Tracy L. Babin/Rodét Slant

Todd-Michael St. Pierre, Cajun/Creole foodie and New Orleans native, is the author of the popular cookbooks *Taste of Tremé* and *Jambalaya, Crawfish Pie, Filé Gumbo!*, He is also author of children's picture books, including *Who Dat Night Before Christmas, Fat Tuesday, Nola and Roux*, and *The Crawfish Family Band*. He has served as a judge for the Reading Rainbow Young Writers and Illustrators Contest and has developed recipes for *Cooking Light* magazine.

Todd-Michael's books have been featured in the *San Francisco Chronicle*, the *Advocate*, the *Times-Picayune*, the *Denver Post*, the *Christian Science Monitor*, the *Daily Meal*, *Southern Living* magazine, *Louisiana Cookin'* magazine, and *AOL Food*. He also contributes to elementary and middle-school textbooks published by Oxford University Press. His website is www.ToddStPierre.com